#71
Westwood Branch
1246 Glendon Ave.
Los Angeles, CA 90024

Easy Beading

Fast. Fashionable. Fun.

Vol. 2

The best projects from the second year of *BeadStyle* magazine

From the editors of *BeadStyle* magazine

KALMBACH BOOKS

Acknowledgments

Linda J. Augsburg, Paulette Biedenbender, Stacy Blint, Mindy Brooks, Naomi Fujimoto, Cathryn Jakicic, Anne Nikolai Kloss, Jane Konkel, Patricia Lantier, Carrie Rohloff, Salena Safranski, Maureen Schimmel, Kristin Schneidler, Candice St. Jacques, Beth Stone, Kristin Sutter, Elizabeth Weber, Lesley Weiss, Wendy Witchner

Printed in China

06 07 08 09 10 11 12 13 14 15   10 9 8 7 6 5 4 3 2

Visit our Web site at
http://kalmbachbooks.com

Secure online ordering available

Publisher's Cataloging-In-Publication Data
(Prepared by The Donohue Group, Inc.)

Easy beading : fast, fashionable, fun : the best projects from the second year of BeadStyle magazine / from the editors of BeadStyle magazine.

    p., : col. ill. ; cm.
    Includes index.
    ISBN: 0-87116-226-1

1. Beadwork--Handbooks, manuals, etc. 2. Beads-- Handbooks, manuals, etc. 3. Jewelry making-- Handbooks, manuals, etc. I. Title: BeadStyle Magazine.

TT860 .E27 2006
745.594/2

ISBN-10: 0-87116-226-1
ISBN-13: 978-0-87116-226-7

Senior art director: Lisa Bergman
Assistant art director: Kelly Katlaps
Book layout: Sabine Beaupré
Photographers: Jim Forbes, William Zuback
Project editors: Tea Benduhn, Karin Buckingham, Julia Gerlach

Contents

Glass and seed beads

Pearls and shells

Metal and chain

Gemstones

Crystals

Mixed media

**Look for great shortcuts
on these pages:**
49, 81, 123, 165, 207, 255

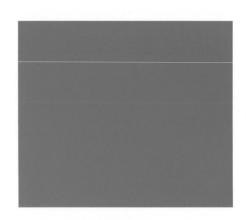

Introduction

Looking through the projects in this book, I feel like I've just bought the "Greatest Hits" CD of my favorite artist and I don't know which song to listen to first. I usually end up listening to the whole thing once all the way through and then going back and playing my *favorite* favorites.

I'd recommend the same approach for this book. You could call it *BeadStyle*'s Greatest Hits – Volume 2.

The number of projects is a bit overwhelming. We've included 125 necklaces, bracelets, and earrings. To make things more manageable, they're organized by materials: Glass and seed beads, pearls and shells, metal and chain, gemstones, crystals, and mixed media.

I'll probably end up reorganizing them for my to-do list into my own categories: Things to make for myself, things to make as gifts, pieces I want to reproduce as shown, and pieces I'll want to tweak a little – to suit my personal color preference or follow a current fashion trend.

I'll also take myself out of the decision-making process a few times by loaning the book to friends as an interactive "gift certificate." I used the first *Easy Beading* that way and friends loved to pick out the gift I would make them. But more often than not, they wanted to keep the book and start making things for themselves.

If you're a beginning beader – congratulations, you've found the perfect book. Each project has been tested by our editors to make sure it can be completed by beaders of all experience levels. We've also included a section of beading terms and basic techniques.

If you've been beading a while, I'd still encourage you to check out the projects inside. At *BeadStyle*, we're working to create more than just easy projects. Each issue (and book) is filled with beautiful, fashionable jewelry that also happens to be accessible to the beginning beader.

And if you're still reading at this point, you're more patient than I am. I would have started to look at the jewelry long before this. You can stop being polite now and start browsing. Have a great time, and I hope you enjoy the projects as much as we did.

Cathy

Cathryn Jakicic
Editor, *BeadStyle* magazine

Beading terms

tools and materials

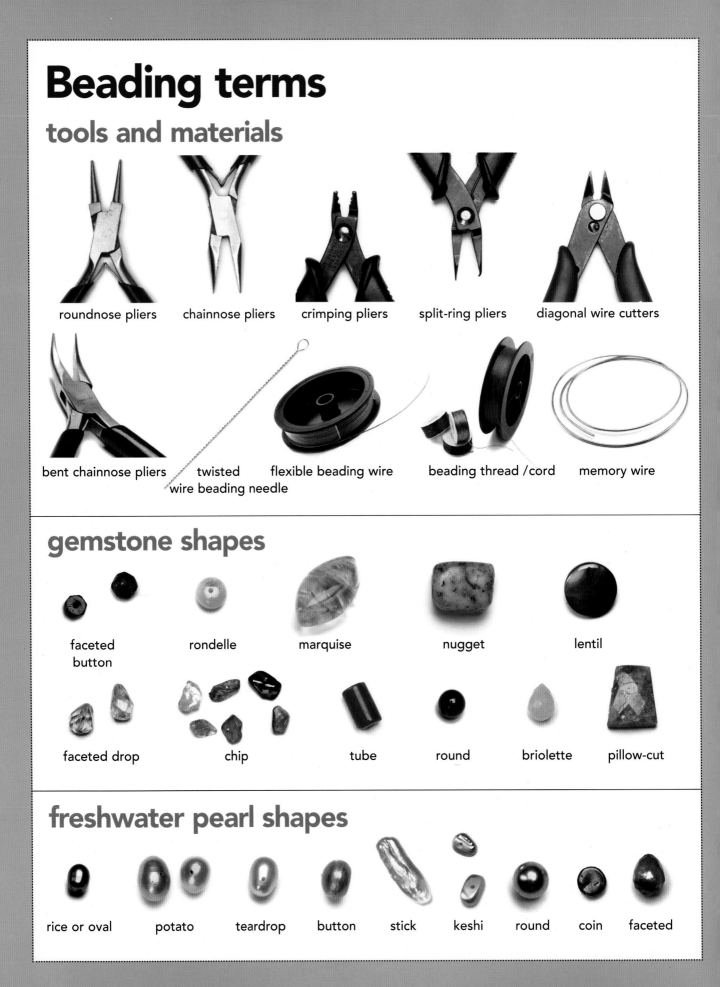

roundnose pliers   chainnose pliers   crimping pliers   split-ring pliers   diagonal wire cutters

bent chainnose pliers   twisted wire beading needle   flexible beading wire   beading thread / cord   memory wire

gemstone shapes

faceted button   rondelle   marquise   nugget   lentil

faceted drop   chip   tube   round   briolette   pillow-cut

freshwater pearl shapes

rice or oval   potato   teardrop   button   stick   keshi   round   coin   faceted

glass, crystal, and miscellaneous beads

| crescent | petal | flowers | millefiori | dichroic glass | Venetian glass |

| bugle beads | twisted bugle beads | rondelles or buttons | faceted button or rondelle | furnace glass | fringe or drop | teardrop |

| Czech fire-polished | cathedral fire-polished | fire-polished drop | bicone crystal | round crystal | cube-shaped crystal | cone-shaped crystal | crystal briolette |

| saucer-shaped crystal | elongated bicone crystal | crystal drop | top-drilled saucer (with jump ring attached) | rhinestone rondelle | rhinestone squaredelle |

   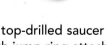

| triangle | cube-shaped | heishe | liquid silver | marcasite | horn | bone |

findings, spacers, and connectors

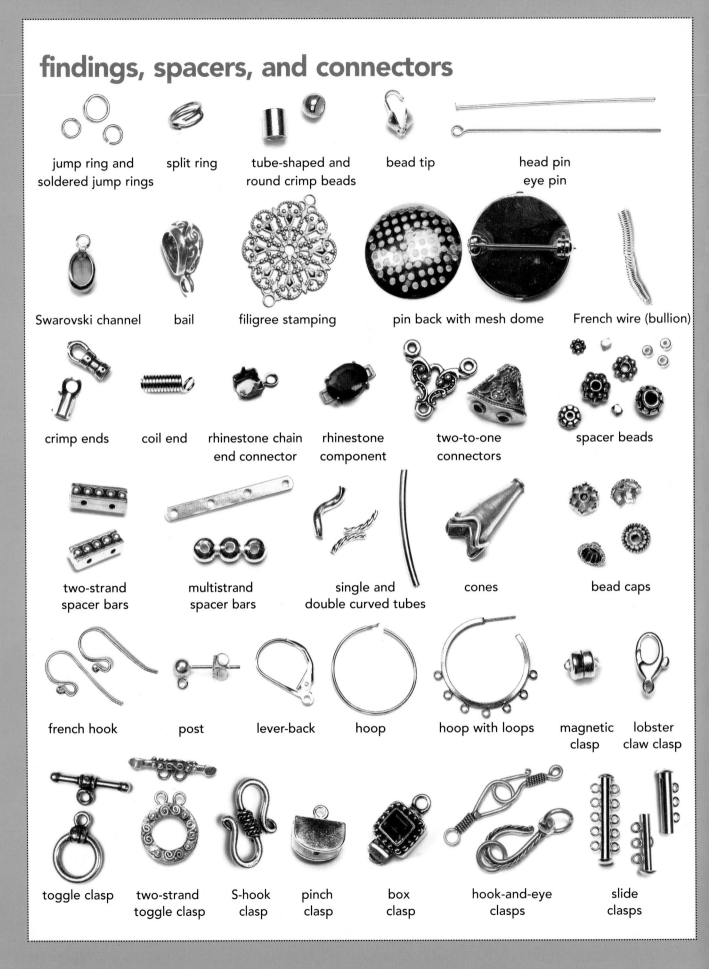

jump ring and
soldered jump rings

split ring

tube-shaped and
round crimp beads

bead tip

head pin
eye pin

Swarovski channel

bail

filigree stamping

pin back with mesh dome

French wire (bullion)

crimp ends

coil end

rhinestone chain
end connector

rhinestone
component

two-to-one
connectors

spacer beads

two-strand
spacer bars

multistrand
spacer bars

single and
double curved tubes

cones

bead caps

french hook

post

lever-back

hoop

hoop with loops

magnetic
clasp

lobster
claw clasp

toggle clasp

two-strand
toggle clasp

S-hook
clasp

pinch
clasp

box
clasp

hook-and-eye
clasps

slide
clasps

Frequently asked questions

Q What are the "must have" supplies for a beginning beader?
There's nothing more frustrating than beginning a project and realizing you don't have the needed materials. Stock your work area with .014 or .015 flexible beading wire, crimp tubes, head pins, an assortment of clasps, split and jump rings, and spacer beads in at least two sizes. Basic tools include diagonal wire cutters, and chainnose and roundnose pliers. You may want a padded work surface, a task lamp, and crimping pliers. Like most of ours, your bead stash will multiply before your eyes!

Q How can I decide what kind of flexible beading wire to use with a project?

The .012, .014, and .015 refers to different diameters of beading wire. For example, .012 wire measures .012 inches in diameter. The weight and design of your project will determine the choice of wire. Generally, use .010 or .012 to string lightweight or small-hole beads; .014 or .015 for most gemstones, crystals, and glass beads; and .018, .019, or .024 to string heavy beads or nuggets. Additionally, wire comes in different strand quantities – 7, 19, 21, and 49. This refers to the number of wires entwined to comprise the diameter. The more strands, the more pliable the wire and the less likely it is that the wire will kink.

Q Can you please explain the difference between seed beads and Japanese cylinder beads?

Seed beads come in a range of sizes, from 6º to 15º. The larger the number, the smaller the bead. The size of the hole and the length of the bead can vary, but the overall diameter is the same. If the directions call for 1½ inches of seed beads, measure your length, instead of counting your beads. Japanese cylinder beads are machine cut and thus more uniform in size and color than seed beads. Delicas are a brand name for Japanese cylinder beads produced by Miyuki; Toho is another manufacturer of cylinder beads. Use cylinder beads when uniformity is important.

Q I have trouble visualizing your projects made with the selection of beads I have at my local shop. Can you give me some tips on adapting a project to different beads?

Be creative! Substitute different types of gemstones, pearls, crystals, or beads based on preference or what is available at your local bead shop. Also, consider trying different shapes – cubes instead of round beads, for example. Keep in mind the size and proportion of the materials used when making substitutions. For example, if a project uses 8mm and 6mm beads, you can recreate it with 10mm and 8mm beads, but the final measurement will increase as well, unless you reduce the bead count. If you use much larger beads, consider using thicker wire and a larger clasp.

Q Can you give advice on choosing crimp sizes and crimping methods?

Both flat and folded crimps provide a strong hold. Folded crimps are preferred when the crimp is noticeable. Also, a folded crimp can slide easily into a large-hole bead for a polished finish. When you make a folded crimp, be sure the wires are separated within the crimp as you make the first fold. Most jewelry can be finished with 1 x 2mm tube crimps. Micro crimps are designed for finer wire or to keep beads stable on illusion necklaces. Flatten a micro crimp with chainnose pliers or a special tool made for micro crimping.

How many beads per inch?

Bead size	3mm	4mm	5mm	6mm	8mm	10mm	12mm
# beads/in.	8.25	6.25	5.0	4.25	3.25	2.5	2.0

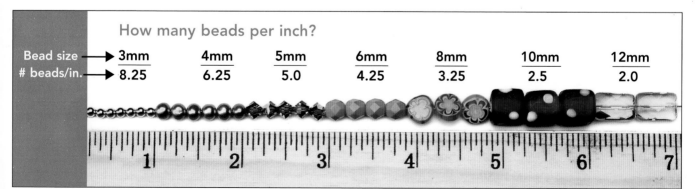

Basic techniques

Learn the key jewelry-making techniques used in bead-stringing projects in this step-by-step reference

flattened crimp

Hold the crimp bead using the tip of your chainnose pliers. Squeeze the pliers firmly to flatten the crimp. Tug the clasp to make sure the crimp has a solid grip on the wire. If the wire slides, remove the crimp bead and repeat the steps with a new crimp bead.

Make sure the flattened crimp is secure.

overhand knot

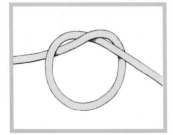

Make a loop and pass the working end through it. Pull the ends to tighten the knot.

folded crimp

Position the crimp bead in the notch closest to the crimping pliers' handle.

Separate the wires and firmly squeeze the crimp.

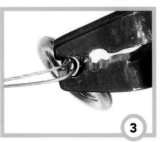

Move the crimp into the notch at the pliers' tip and hold the crimp as shown. Squeeze the crimp bead, folding it in half at the indentation.

Tug the clasp to make sure the folded crimp is secure.

folded crimp end

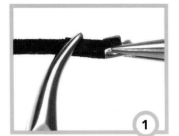

Glue one end of the cord and place it in a crimp end. Use chainnose pliers to fold one side of the crimp end over the cord.

Repeat on the second side and squeeze gently.

surgeon's knot

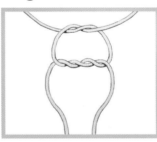

Cross the right end over the left and go under and over the cord. Go under and over the cord again. Pull the ends to tighten. Cross the left end over the right end and go through once. Tighten.

plain loop

Trim the wire ⅜ in. (1cm) above the top bead. Make a right angle bend close to the bead.

Grab the wire's tip with roundnose pliers. Roll the wire to form a half circle. Release the wire.

Reposition the pliers in the loop and continue rolling, forming a centered circle above the bead.

The finished loop should have a nice, round shape.

wrapped loop

1 Make sure you have at least 1¼ in. (3.2cm) of wire above the bead. With the tip of your chainnose pliers, grasp the wire directly above the bead. Bend the wire (above the pliers) into a right angle.

2 Using roundnose pliers, position the jaws in the bend.

3 Bring the wire over the top jaw of the roundnose pliers.

4 Reposition the pliers' lower jaw snugly into the loop. Curve the wire downward around the bottom of the roundnose pliers. This is the first half of a wrapped loop.

5 Position the chainnose pliers' jaws across the loop.

6 Wrap the wire around the wire stem, covering the stem between the loop and the top bead. Trim the excess wire and press the cut end close to the wraps with chainnose pliers.

wrapping above a top-drilled bead

1 Center a top-drilled bead on a 3-in. (7.6cm) piece of wire. Bend each wire upward to form a squared-off "U" shape.

2 Cross the wires into an "X" above the bead.

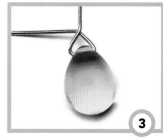

3 Using chainnose pliers, make a small bend in each wire so the ends form a right angle.

4 Wrap the horizontal wire around the vertical wire as in a wrapped loop. Trim the excess wire.

split rings

1 To open, slide the hooked tip of split-ring pliers between the two overlapping wires.

jump rings

1 Hold the jump ring with two pairs of chainnose pliers or chainnose and roundnose pliers, as shown.

2 To open the jump ring, bring one pair of pliers toward you and push the other pair away.

3 String materials on the open jump ring. Reverse the steps to close. ❖

Glass and

seed beads

by Eva Kapitany

Take advantage of the many beautiful dichroic beads available to make an easy-to-string bracelet. Vibrant crystals, spaced evenly throughout the piece, boost the beads' brilliance and add a touch of elegance. The bracelet's simple and versatile design makes it a welcome addition to a casual wardrobe or a radiant accessory for evening wear.

Jewel tones

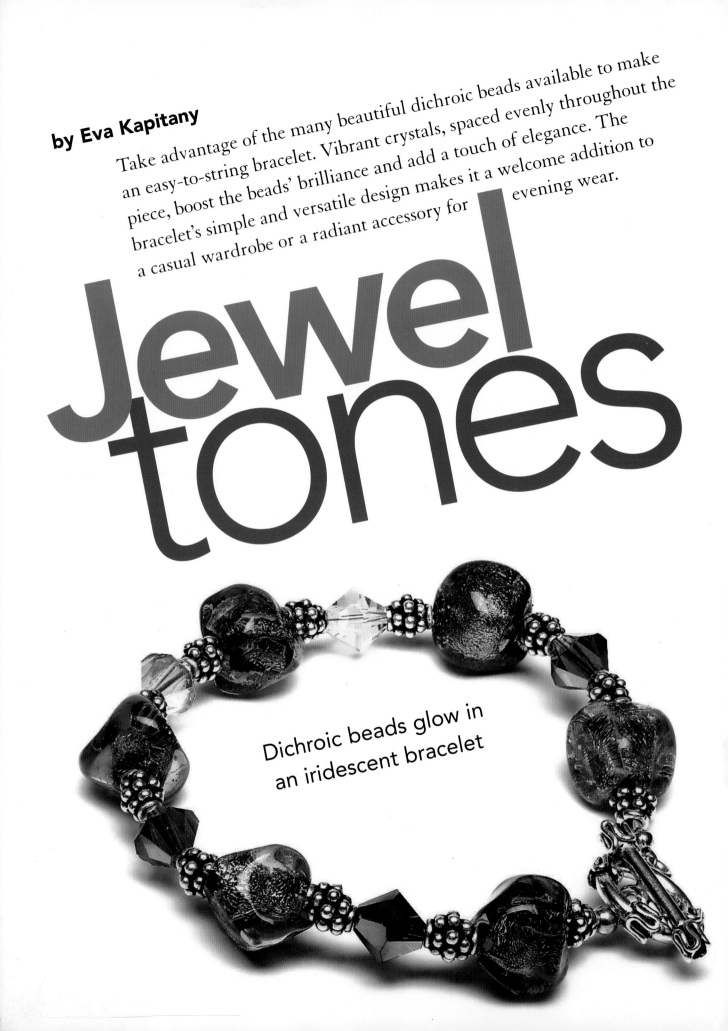

Dichroic beads glow in an iridescent bracelet

A

1. Determine the finished length of your bracelet. Add 5 in. (13cm) and cut a piece of beading wire to that length.

2. String a crimp bead, a 3mm round spacer, and half the clasp. Go back through the beads but do not crimp the crimp bead yet.

B

3. String a 5mm cone-shaped bead (if using bicones) or a 4 x 5mm silver bead (if using cubes) covering the wire's tail.

C

4. String a dichroic bead, a 5 x 6mm or 4 x 5mm silver bead, a crystal, and a silver bead.

Repeat this pattern until the bracelet is within ½ in. (1.3cm) of the desired length. End with a cone-shaped bead or a silver bead.

Repeat step 2 with the remaining clasp half. Tighten the wire, check the fit, and add or remove beads from each end if necessary. Crimp the crimp beads (Basic Techniques, p. 12) and trim the excess wire. ❖

Contact Eva in care of BeadStyle.

> **EDITOR'S TIP**
> The use of AB-finish crystals enhances the dichroic beads' iridescent features.

Supply List

both projects
- flexible beading wire, .014 or .015
- chainnose or crimping pliers
- diagonal wire cutters

dichroic and bicone crystal bracelet
- **6** 11 x 12mm dichroic beads (Paula Radke, 800-341-4945, beaduse.com)
- **5** 12mm bicone crystals
- **10** 5 x 6mm silver beads
- **2** 3 x 5mm cone-shaped silver beads

- **2** 3mm round spacer beads
- **2** crimp beads
- **toggle clasp

dichroic and crystal cube bracelet
- **6** 9 x 15mm dichroic beads (Dee Howl Beads, 505-772-2634, deehowlbeads@gilanet.com)
- **6** 12mm cube-shaped crystals
- **13** 4 x 5mm silver beads
- **2** 3mm round spacer beads
- **2** crimp beads
- **toggle clasp

Bold and beautiful

Dangles swing from a coiled cuff • by Heather Powers

A flat multihole bead or spacer is the perfect unifying – and stabilizing – element for coiled memory wire. The polymer clay bead here, mixed with several sizes and colors of seed beads, an eclectic mix of dangles, and a few accent beads, produced this bold cuff bracelet.

1. String a 6mm accent bead onto a head pin; repeat with the remaining 6mm beads, adding a 2mm spacer bead on one. String a 4mm accent bead and a flat spacer onto a head pin. Trim the head pins to ⅜ in. (1cm) above the beads and turn a plain loop (Basic Techniques, p. 12). Set aside.

2. To make a sixth dangle out of wire, trim the end off a head pin. Use roundnose and chainnose pliers to turn a spiral design. Make a plain loop above the spiral. Set aside.

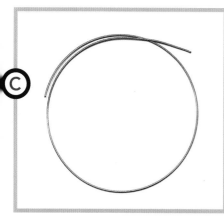

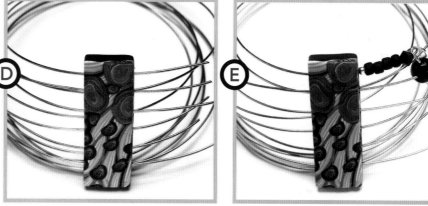

3. Use heavy-duty wire cutters to cut six 1⅓-coil pieces of memory wire. On each piece, use chainnose pliers to straighten the curve about 1 in. (2.5cm) from one end.

4. String the straightened end of each piece of memory wire through the art bead.

5. String a 2mm bead and ½ in. (1.3cm) of seed beads, ending with a 4mm accent bead. Turn a plain loop at the end of the memory wire. Open the loop on a dangle, attach it to the memory-wire loop, and close the dangle's loop.

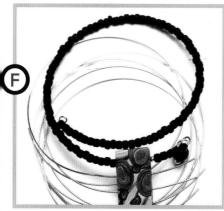

6. On the other end of the wire, string a 2mm bead. String seed beads on the rest of the coil and turn a plain loop at the end. Repeat steps 5 and 6 with the remaining five coils of memory wire, varying the sizes and colors of beads.

7. Snip the end from a head pin and turn a loop or coil at the end. Slide the pin through the six free loops on the bracelet and turn a matching loop at the other end. ✣

Supply List

- 6-hole art bead (Heather Powers, humblebeads.com)
- 5g size 8º seed beads, four colors
- 3g size 11º seed beads, two colors
- **13** 2mm spacer beads
- **4** 6mm accent beads or crystals
- **7** 4mm accent beads or crystals
- 4mm flat spacer bead
- **7** 2-in. (5.1cm) head pins
- memory wire, bracelet diameter
- chainnose and roundnose pliers
- diagonal wire cutters
- heavy-duty wire cutters

Heather, a polymer clay bead artist, offers kits for this project. Contact her through humblebeads.com.

Brighten any day with jewelry in
luscious shades of sunny yellow or ocean
blue, accented with juicy peach or turquoise
glass teardrops. Try teardrops with an AB or
two-tone finish, strung so the finish shows on
the front of the necklace. Matching gemstone
or glass chips are available in virtually
every color – any will work well
for a playful set.

Matched set

Create a pastel necklace, bracelet, and earrings with gemstone chips and glass teardrops • **by Erika Barrientes**

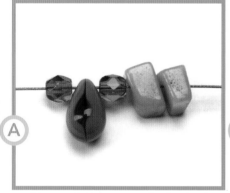

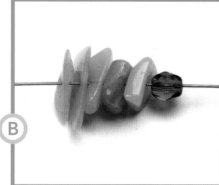

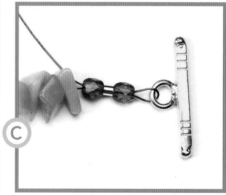

necklace • 1. Determine the finished length of your necklace. (This one is 20 in./51cm.) Add 6 in. (15cm) and cut a piece of beading wire to that length.

String a 4mm crystal, a teardrop, a crystal, and two chips. Repeat eight times. String a crystal, a teardrop, and a crystal.

2. On each end, string five chips and a crystal. Repeat four or more times on each end, until the necklace is within 1 in. (2.5cm) of the desired length. Since chips are irregular, make sure both sides of the necklace are the same length.

3. On one end, string a crimp bead, a crystal, and half the clasp. Go back through the beads just strung plus one or two more and tighten the wire. Repeat on the other end. Check the fit, and add or remove beads from each end, if necessary. Crimp the crimp beads (Basic Techniques, p. 12) and trim the excess wire.

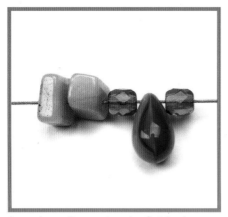

bracelet • Determine the finished length of your bracelet, add 5 in. (13cm), and cut a piece of beading wire to that length. String two chips, a crystal, a teardrop, and a crystal. Repeat until the bracelet is within 1 in. of the desired length. End with two chips. Check the fit and attach the clasp as in step 3 of the necklace.

Supply List

necklace
- 16-in. (41cm) strand 6-8mm gemstone or glass chips
- **10** 6 x 9mm glass teardrops, top-drilled
- **30-40** 4mm Czech fire-polished crystals
- flexible beading wire, .014 or .015
- **2** crimp beads
- clasp
- chainnose or crimping pliers
- diagonal wire cutters

bracelet
- chips left over from necklace
- **8-10** 6 x 9mm glass teardrops, top-drilled
- **16-22** 4mm Czech fire-polished crystals
- flexible beading wire, .014 or .015
- **2** crimp beads
- clasp
- chainnose or crimping pliers
- diagonal wire cutters

earrings
- chips left over from necklace
- **2** 10-13mm disc-shaped beads
- **4** 4mm Czech fire-polished crystals
- **2** 2-in. (5cm) head pins
- pair of earring wires or posts
- chainnose and roundnose pliers
- diagonal wire cutters

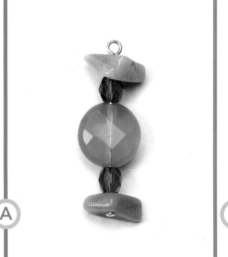

(A)

earrings • **1.** String a chip, a crystal, a disc, a crystal, and a chip on a head pin. Make a plain loop (Basic Techniques) above the bead.

(B)

2. Open the loop on an earring wire and attach the dangle. Close the loop. Make a second earring to match the first. ❖

Contact Erika at erikabarrientes@ hotmail.com.

Summer simplicity

String a slender necklace in under 20 minutes

by Yvette Jones

Rounds, rondelles, and bugles make this necklace a great accessory that's simple to assemble. All the elements are available in a multitude of colors; classic silver and apple green are but two of your options. So make a bunch in bright colors to pair with your favorite outfits.

SupplyList

- **5** 8-10mm round beads
- **6** 6-7mm rhinestone rondelles
- **3g** size 3 (6mm) twisted bugle beads
- **4** 2-3mm round spacer beads
- flexible beading wire, .014 or .015
- **2** crimp beads
- lobster claw clasp and soldered jump ring
- chainnose or crimping pliers
- diagonal wire cutters

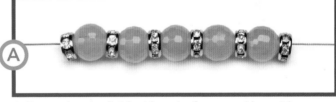

1. Determine the finished length of your necklace. (These are 16 in. and 18 in./41cm and 46cm, respectively.) Add 6 in. (15cm) and cut a piece of beading wire to that length. Alternate six rhinestone rondelles with five round beads on the wire. Center the beads on the wire.

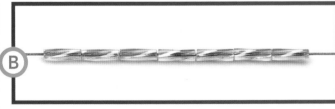

2. String an equal number of bugle beads on each end until the necklace is within 1 in. (2.5cm) of the desired length.

Contact Yvette at Chic Designs by Yvette, (914) 450-3046 or ymaddux@juno.com.

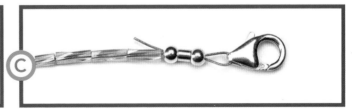

3. On one end, string a round spacer, a crimp bead, a spacer, and the clasp. Go back through the beads just strung and tighten the wire. Repeat on the other end, substituting a jump ring for the clasp. Check the fit, and add or remove beads from each end if necessary. Crimp the crimp beads (Basic Techniques, p. 12) and trim the excess wire. ❖

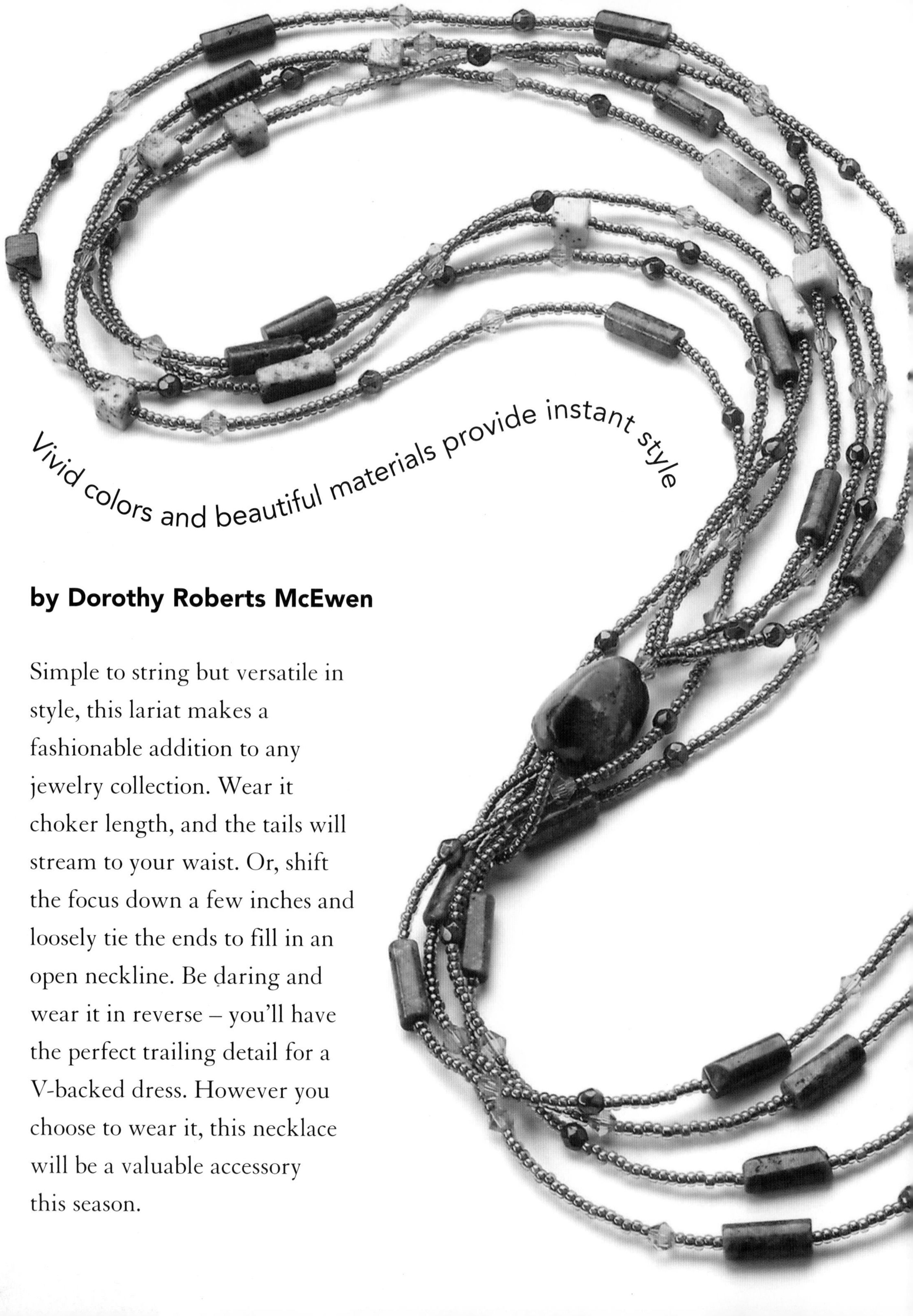

Vivid colors and beautiful materials provide instant style

by Dorothy Roberts McEwen

Simple to string but versatile in style, this lariat makes a fashionable addition to any jewelry collection. Wear it choker length, and the tails will stream to your waist. Or, shift the focus down a few inches and loosely tie the ends to fill in an open neckline. Be daring and wear it in reverse – you'll have the perfect trailing detail for a V-backed dress. However you choose to wear it, this necklace will be a valuable accessory this season.

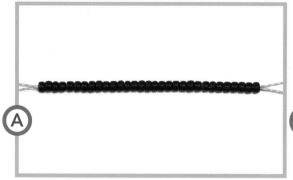

1. Cut two 65-in. (1.7m) pieces of beading wire. String approximately 30 size 11º seed beads over both wires. Center the beads on the wires.

2. String a crimp bead over all four wires. Pull the ends to form a loop. Check the size of the loop to be sure the accent beads fit through. Add or remove beads, if necessary. Make a folded crimp (Basic Techniques, p. 12).

3. String the focal bead over the four strands, covering the folded crimp.

4. Separate the wires and begin stringing seed beads and accent beads, staggering the placement of similar beads from strand to strand. Bead each strand until it is within 2 in. (5cm) of the desired length. (These strands extend 29½ in./ 75cm beyond the focal bead.) If desired, vary the lengths of the strands.

Long lariat

5. String a crimp bead, 6-10 seed beads, an accent bead, and a seed bead. Repeat on the remaining three strands.

6. Go around the seed bead and back through the accent bead, the seed beads, the crimp bead, and a few more seed beads. Repeat on the remaining three strands.

7. Tighten the wires and check the fit. Add or remove beads, if necessary. Make a folded crimp on each strand and trim the excess wire. ✤

SupplyList

- 20mm (approx.) large-hole focal bead
- **50-60** 4-8mm accent beads, assorted shapes
- **10-20** 4mm round crystals, color matching accent beads
- **10-15** 4mm bicone crystals, color matching seed beads
- 7-10g seed beads, size 8º
- 7-10g seed beads, size 11º
- flexible beading wire, .014 or .015
- 5 crimp beads
- crimping pliers
- diagonal wire cutters

Contact Dorothy in care of BeadStyle.

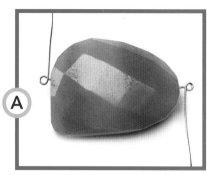

1. Cut a 5-in. (13cm) piece of 22- or 24-gauge wire. String the pendant and make the first half of a wrapped loop (Basic Techniques, p. 12) on each end.

2. Determine the finished length of your necklace. (The aqua necklace is 16 in./41 cm; the pink, 18 in./46cm; the lavender, 21 in./53cm.) Subtract 1 in. (2.5cm) and cut a piece of chain to that length. Cut the chain in half. Attach an end link of each piece to a pendant loop and complete the wraps.

3. Check the fit, allowing 1 in. for the clasp. Trim an equal number of links from each end if necessary.
   Open a jump ring (Basic Techniques). Attach an end link to a clasp half. Close the jump ring. Repeat on the other end. ❖

Contact Diana at jewels@deenmiele.com.

Facet
by Diana Grossman

fascination

Accent a simple necklace with a chunky pendant

Chunky, faceted glass is the focus of this simple necklace. Dangled from fine cable chain, the pendant needs no embellishment to dazzle. Wear two necklaces in different colors and lengths for up-to-the-minute style.

SupplyList

- faceted pendant, approx. 30 x 40mm
- 5 in. (13cm) 22- or 24-gauge wire, half hard
- 16-22 in. (41-56cm) cable chain, 1.5-2.5mm links
- 2 3-4mm jump rings
- toggle clasp
- chainnose and roundnose pliers
- diagonal wire cutters

Garden

Create a botanical
bracelet and
blossom earrings

variety

by Beth Stone

Everyone knows the mood-boosting properties of fresh-cut flowers. Since absconding with a bouquet from the garden next door is generally frowned upon, string a fabulous wrist corsage and earrings instead. Colorful flower beads will evoke a positive disposition in you and keep relations amicable with your neighbors, too.

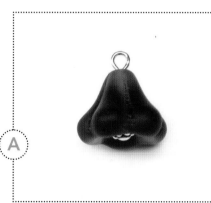

bracelet • **1.** String a 3mm flat spacer and a flower bead on a head pin. Make a plain loop (Basic Techniques, p. 12) above the bead.

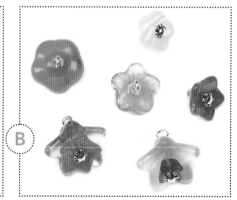

2. Make a total of 30-36 flower units. If desired, string a flat spacer, a small flower, and a 14mm flower on several of the head pins.

3. Determine the finished length of your bracelet, add 5 in. (13cm), and cut a piece of beading wire to that length. String a pearl and a flower unit. Repeat until the bracelet is within 1 in. (2.5cm) of the desired length, ending with a pearl.

4. On each end, string a 3 x 5mm spacer, an accent bead, a crimp bead, an accent bead, and half the clasp. Go back through the last beads strung. Tighten the wires, check the fit, and add or remove beads, if necessary. Crimp the crimp beads (Basic Techniques) and trim the excess wire.

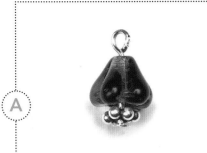

A

B

C

earrings • **1.** String a 3mm spacer and a 5mm flower bead on a head pin. Make a plain loop above the bead. Make a total of seven flower units.

2. Trim the head from a head pin and make a plain loop at one end. Or, use an eye pin. Open the loop, attach the 5mm flower unit, and close the loop.

3. String a 14mm flower bead on the eye pin. Make a plain loop above the bead.

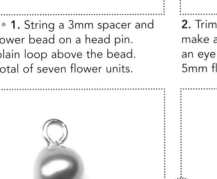

D

E

F

4. Trim the head from a head pin and make a plain loop at one end. Or, use an eye pin. String a pearl. Make a plain loop above the bead. Make a second pearl unit.

5. Open one of the pearl unit's loops and attach it to the other pearl unit. Close the loop.

Open a jump ring (Basic Techniques) and string three 5mm flower units, the 14mm flower dangle, three 5mm flower units, and one loop on the connected pearl unit. Close the jump ring.

6. Open the loop on an earring wire and attach the dangle. Close the loop. Make a second earring to match the first. ❧

Contact Beth at (248) 855-9358 or bnshdl@msn.com.

Supply List

both projects
- chainnose and roundnose pliers
- diagonal wire cutters

bracelet
- **30-45** 5-14mm flower-shaped beads
- 16-in. (41cm) strand 4mm potato pearls
- **30-36** 3mm flat spacers
- **2** 3 x 5mm spacers
- **4** 3mm accent beads
- **30-36** 1½-in. (3.8cm) head pins

- flexible beading wire, .014 or .015
- **2** crimp beads
- toggle clasp

earrings
- **14** 5mm flower-shaped beads
- **2** 14mm flower-shaped beads
- **4** 4mm pearls
- **14** 3mm flat spacers
- **20** 1½-in. head pins or **14** 1½-in. head pins and **6** 1½-in. eye pins
- pair of decorative earring wires

Briolette beauty

Suspend a teardrop pendant from a three-strand necklace

by Christianne Camera

The focus of this necklace is a light-catching briolette, in colors such as aquamarine, purple, and sand. Satin finish and hex-cut seed beads create contrasting textures among the strands. You'll love this project's simplicity and reasonable price tag.

SupplyList

- briolette, approx. 16 x 25mm (Eclectica, 262-641-0910, eclecticabeads.com)
- 16-in. (41cm) strand 2-4mm glass or gemstone beads, or 5g size 8º hex-cut seed beads
- 5g size 10º seed beads, satin finish
- 5g size 11º Japanese cylinder beads
- **2** 4mm bicone crystals or size 8º seed beads
- flexible beading wire, .012 or .014
- 3 in. (7.6cm) 22-gauge wire, half hard
- **6** crimp beads
- three-strand clasp
- chainnose and roundnose pliers
- diagonal wire cutters
- crimping pliers (optional)

Contact Christianne in care of BeadStyle.

A **1.** Cut a 3-in. (7.6cm) piece of 22-gauge wire. String the briolette and wrap it as for a top-drilled bead (Basic Techniques, p. 12). Make a wrapped loop above the wraps.

B  **2.** Determine the finished length of your necklace. (These are 16½ in./42cm.) Add 6 in. (15cm) and cut three pieces of beading wire to that length. Center a crystal or size 8º seed bead, a cylinder bead, the pendant, and a crystal or size 8º seed bead on all three strands.

C  **3.** On one wire, string cylinder beads on each side of the pendant until the strand is within 1 in. (2.5cm) of the desired length. On the second wire, string 2-4mm beads or hex-cut beads. On the third wire, string size 10º seed beads. Each strand should be the same length.

D  **4.** On each end of each strand, string a crimp bead, a seed bead, and the respective loop on a clasp half. Go back through the last beads strung and tighten the wires. Check the fit, and add or remove an equal number of beads from each end, if necessary. Crimp the crimp beads (Basic Techniques) and trim the excess wire. ❖

Every picture tells a story, and cancelled foreign stamps can take you on an exciting visual journey. Imagine the fascinating stories or news these stamps carried to faraway places over the years. Dream about fantastic tales as you string a framed stamp on a strand of rondelles to enhance the stamp's detailed artistry. Your necklace will forever hold your secret dreams of travel and adventure.

First-class

1. Determine the finished length of your necklace. (These are 17 in./43cm with 1½-in./3.8cm extenders.) Add 6 in. (15cm) and cut a piece of flexible beading wire to that length. Center the pendant on the wire.

String seven rondelles and a flat spacer on each end. Repeat this pattern until the necklace is within 1 in. (2.5cm) of the desired length.

2. String a crimp bead, a 3mm round, and a 1½-in. piece of chain on one end. Go back through the beads just strung and one rondelle.

Repeat on the other end of the necklace, substituting a lobster claw or hook clasp for the chain. Tighten the wire. Check the fit, and add or remove an equal number of beads from each end if necessary. Crimp the crimp beads (Basic Techniques, p. 12) and trim the excess wire.

SupplyList

both projects
- flexible beading wire, .014 or .015
- chainnose and roundnose pliers
- diagonal wire cutters

multicolored necklace
- framed stamp pendant (Eclectica, 262-641-0910, eclecticabeads.com)
- 3 or 4 6-in. (15cm) strands 4mm Czech fire-polished faceted rondelles
- **20-24** 4mm flat spacer beads
- **2** 3mm round spacer beads
- **2** crimp beads
- 1½-in. (3.8cm) head pin
- 1½-in. 3mm chain
- lobster claw clasp

blue necklace
- framed stamp pendant (Eclectica)
- **1** or **2** 16-in. (41cm) strands 3mm faceted rondelles, iolite
- **20-24** 4mm flat spacer beads
- **2** 3mm round spacer beads
- **2** crimp beads
- 1½-in. head pin
- 1½-in. 3mm chain
- hook clasp

3. To make an extender dangle, string a rondelle on a head pin. Make the first half of a wrapped loop (Basic Techniques) above the bead.

4. Attach the dangle's loop to the chain's end link. Complete the wraps. ❖

Contact Irina at (262) 641-0910 or at info@eclecticabeads.com.

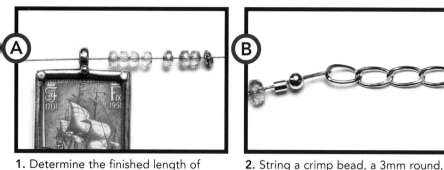

by **Irina Miech**

fantasy

Frame a stamp pendant with a delicate necklace

Crystals and crescents

Uncommon shapes meet in a curvaceous necklace

by Eva Kapitany

Giving the illusion of a stacked arrangement, the repeating contours in this distinctive necklace contribute to its appeal. Crescent-shaped beads and crystal drops are available in limited size and color combinations, yet appealing bead alternatives abound. Consider pairing hearts with teardrops, bell-shaped flowers with daggers, or petals with faceted drops.

Contact Eva in care of BeadStyle.

1. Determine the finished length of your necklace. (These are 15½ in./39cm.) Add 6 in. (15cm) and cut a piece of beading wire to that length. Center a drop on the wire.

2. On each side of the drop, string four crescents or petals and a drop, so the shapes face opposite directions on each side of the center drop. Repeat this pattern until the strand is within 1 in. (2.5cm) of the desired length. End with a crescent or petal.

3. On each end, string a bicone, round spacer, crimp bead, round spacer, and half the clasp. Go back through the beads just strung and tighten the wire. Check the fit, and add or remove beads from each end, if necessary. Crimp the crimp beads (Basic Techniques, p. 12). Trim the excess wire. ❖

SupplyList

- **64-72** 6 x 14mm crescent- or petal-shaped glass beads (Eclectica, 262-641-0910)
- **15-17** faceted drop crystals, 11 x 5.5mm or 13 x 6.5mm
- **2** 6mm bicone crystals
- **4** 2-3mm round spacer beads
- flexible beading wire, .014 or .015
- **2** crimp beads
- box clasp
- chainnose or crimping pliers
- diagonal wire cutters

Jazzy trio

Spotlight three art beads in a multistrand chip and seed bead bracelet

by Anne Nikolai Kloss

Art beads traditionally are large one-of-a-kind pieces that serve as focal points. However, many glass artists create art bead sets with subtle variations, offering wider design possibilities. An airy setting of Japanese seed beads and gemstone chips enhances these bold bracelets. Effortless stringing and readily available materials make it easy to alter the color palette to complement your choice of focal beads.

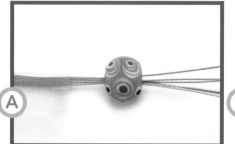

aqua bracelet • 1. Determine the finished length of your bracelet and add 10 in. (25cm). Cut six pieces of beading wire to that length. Center an art bead over all six strands. Tape the strands together on one side of the bead.

2. On the other side of the art bead, beginning with gemstone chips, string 1½ in. (3.8cm) of randomly spaced seed beads and chips on each strand. End with a chip.

3. Loosely braid the strands.

4. String an art bead over all six strands and pull the strands taut.

Remove the tape and repeat steps 2 through 4 on the other side.

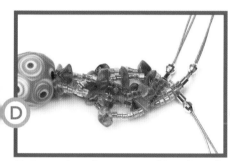

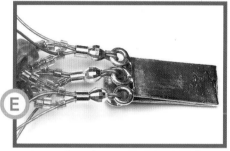

5. On each end, string seed beads and chips until the bracelet is within ½ in. (1.3cm) of the desired length. End with seed beads.

6. Divide the strands into pairs. String a crimp bead and a 3mm round on each pair. Loosely braid the strands.

7. On each end, string each pair of strands through the loops of one clasp half. Go back through the last two beads strung. Tighten the wires, check the fit, and add or remove an equal number of beads from each end, if necessary.

Separate the strands and go through the adjacent seed bead. Crimp the crimp beads (Basic Techniques, p. 12) and trim the excess wire.

black bracelet • 1. Follow steps 1 through 4 of the aqua bracelet using four pieces of beading wire.

2. Follow steps 5 and 6, but loosely braid the strands before dividing them into pairs.

3. Follow step 7 using a two-strand clasp to finish the bracelet. ✤

Supply List

- **3** coordinating art glass beads, approx. 12-15mm
- 16-in. (41cm) strand 4-6mm gemstone chips
- 5g size 14º Japanese seed beads or size 11º Japanese cylinder beads
- **6** 3mm round large-hole beads
- flexible beading wire, .010
- **6** crimp beads
- two- or three-strand clasp
- chainnose or crimping pliers
- diagonal wire cutters

Contact Anne at annekloss@mac.com.

Colorful creation

by Irina Miech

Infused with color, Karen Judt's glass beads dazzle amid a setting of crystals and silver spacers. The necklace, bracelet, and earrings combine assorted colors of glass beads with panache; don't be afraid to string mismatched shades of crystals to heighten the kaleidoscopic effect. If you've been waiting for the right project to use specialty beads, these spirited pieces provide a perfect opportunity to create beautiful jewelry you can treasure.

necklace • 1. Determine the finished length of your necklace. (This one is 17½ in./44.5cm.) Subtract 4 in. (10cm), divide the number in half, and cut two pieces of chain to that length. Cut a 6-in. (15cm) piece of flexible beading wire. String a crimp bead and the end link of a chain segment. Go back through the bead, tighten the wire, and crimp the crimp bead (Basic Techniques, p. 12).

2. String a bead cap, crystal, bead cap, spacer, glass bead, and a spacer, covering the wire tail. Repeat twice, then string a bead cap, a crystal, and a bead cap.

3. String a crimp bead and an end link of the remaining chain segment. Go back through the last few beads strung, tighten the wire, and crimp the crimp bead. Trim the excess wire.

4. Check the fit. If necessary, trim each chain segment so the necklace is within 1 in. (2.5cm) of the desired length. On each end, attach a split ring (Basic Techniques) and half the clasp.

Frame vibrant art beads and crystals with Bali silver for three sensational pieces

bracelet • 1. Determine the finished length of your bracelet, add 5 in. (13cm), and cut a piece of beading wire to that length. String a crimp bead, a round spacer, and half the clasp. Go back through the beads, tighten the wire, and crimp the crimp bead.

2. String a bead cap, crystal, bead cap, 6-8mm spacer, glass bead, and spacer. Repeat five or six times, ending with a bead cap, crystal, and bead cap. Check the fit, and add or remove beads, if necessary. Finish the bracelet as in step 1, going back through an additional bead or two. Trim the excess wire.

Supply List

necklace
- **3** lampwork glass beads, approx. 10 x 13mm (Karen Judt, karenbeads.com)
- **4** 6mm round crystals
- **6** spacers, approx. 3 x 8mm
- **8** 6mm bead caps
- **13-15** in. (33-38cm) chain, approx. 5mm links
- flexible beading wire, .014 or .015
- **2** crimp beads
- **2** split rings
- toggle clasp
- chainnose or crimping pliers
- diagonal wire cutters
- split-ring pliers (optional)

bracelet
- **6-7** lampwork glass beads, approx. 10 x 13mm
- **7-8** 6mm round crystals
- **12-14** spacers, approx. 3 x 8mm
- **14-16** 6mm bead caps
- **2** 2-3mm round spacer beads
- flexible beading wire, .014 or .015
- **2** crimp beads
- toggle clasp
- chainnose or crimping pliers
- diagonal wire cutters

earrings
- **2** lampwork glass beads, approx. 10 x 13mm
- **6** 4mm bicone crystals
- **4** spacers, approx. 3 x 8mm
- **2** flat 6-8mm spacers (optional)
- **2** 2-in. (5cm) head pins or eye pins
- **6** 1-in. (2.5cm) head pins
- pair of earring wires
- chainnose and roundnose pliers
- diagonal wire cutters

earrings • 1. String a crystal on a 1-in. (2.5cm) head pin and make a plain loop (Basic Techniques) above the crystal. Make a total of six dangles and set aside.

2. Trim the end from a 2-in. (5cm) head pin and make a plain loop at one end. Or, use an eye pin. String a flat spacer (if desired), a 3 x 8mm spacer, a glass bead, and a 3 x 8mm spacer. Make a plain loop above the top spacer.

3. Open a loop on the glass-bead dangle and string three crystal dangles. Close the loop.

4. Open the top loop and attach an earring wire. Close the loop. Make a second earring to match the first. ❖

Irina offers kits with similar beads for the necklace, bracelet, and earrings. Contact her at Eclectica, (262) 641-0910 or info@eclecticabeads.com.

by Naomi Fujimoto

Sowing the seeds

Make an easy and colorful choker

Sprinkle assorted seed beads in a bowl, string them with a few gemstone chips, add a clasp, and *voilà,* your necklace is ready to wear. To further simplify stringing, buy premixed assortments of seed beads on hanks and run your beading wire through individual strands. You also can blend your own mix by adding different amounts of each seed bead color. Keep the delicate look of the seed beads in mind when selecting your accent beads.

1. Determine the finished length of your necklace. (The gemstone chip necklaces are 15 in./38cm; the yellow jasper necklace, 16 in./41cm.) Add 6 in. (15cm) and cut a piece of beading wire to that length. Center an accent bead on the wire. If you have more than one accent bead, string a few seed beads between each.

2. Using the end of the beading wire to pick up beads, string assorted seed beads on each end until you are within 1 in. (2.5cm) of the desired length.

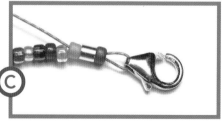

3. String a crimp bead, a seed bead, and the clasp. Go back through the beads just strung and tighten the wire. Repeat on the other end, substituting a soldered jump ring for the clasp. Check the fit and add or remove beads from each end, if necessary. Crimp the crimp beads (Basic Techniques, p. 12) and trim the excess wire. ❖

Supply List

- 5g size 11º seed beads, assorted colors
- assorted gemstone chips or accent beads
- flexible beading wire, .014 or .015
- **2** crimp beads
- lobster claw clasp and soldered jump ring
- chainnose or crimping pliers
- diagonal wire cutters

Gorgeous

by Corrie Haight

Sculpt a fabulous cuff with curved art glass beads and wire

Not for the faint of heart, this colorful cuff fits the bill when you're seeking a bold, confident piece of jewelry. Even though the art glass beads are the focus, the accents are equally important: Bright crystals or textured Hill Tribes silver enhance the beads' ribbons of color and act as spacers. To determine the look and fit without overworking the actual bracelet wire, string a temporary bead arrangement on a lightweight wire. After transferring the beads and finishing a custom clasp, you'll be ready to show off your curves in a one-of-a-kind bracelet.

SupplyList

- **2-3** glass bracelet curves, approx. 1¼-2¾ in. (3-7cm) in length (Olive Glass, oliveglass.com)
- **3-6** 6-15mm accent beads, holes large enough to accommodate 16-gauge wire
- **6-8** 5-8mm large-hole spacers (optional)
- 18 in. (46cm) 16-gauge wire
- 1 ft. (30cm) 20-gauge copper or craft wire
- chainnose and roundnose pliers
- diagonal wire cutters

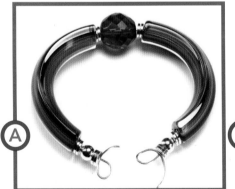

1. Cut a 9-in. (23cm) piece of copper or craft wire. String accent beads, bracelet curves, and spacers (if desired) on the wire. Begin and end with an accent bead or spacer. Make a temporary loop at each end of the wire. Check the fit, allowing 1 in. (2.5cm) for the clasp. Add or remove beads from each end, if necessary. Set aside.

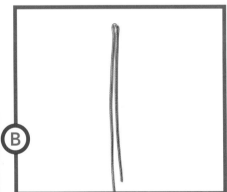

2. Cut an 18-in. (46cm) piece of 16-gauge wire. Bend the wire down approximately 3 in. (7.6cm) from one end.

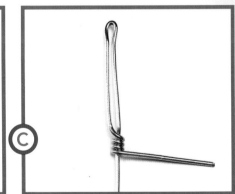

3. Cross the shorter wire over the stem approximately 1¼ in. (3.2cm) from the fold. Wrap the bent piece around the stem two or three times, as in a wrapped loop. Trim the excess wire close to the wraps.

glass

D

4. Use the largest part of your roundnose pliers to curve the loop downward. With chainnose pliers, bend the tip of the fold outward slightly. Gently pinch the two wires together with chainnose pliers.

E

5. Remove the beads from the temporary wire. Carefully string your pattern on the 16-gauge wire, beginning and ending with an accent bead or spacer. Curve the wire slightly to help ease it through the glass beads.

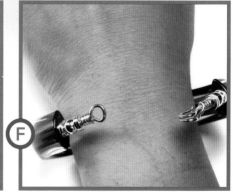

F

6. Make a wrapped loop (Basic Techniques, p. 12) large enough to accommodate the hook closure. Trim the excess wire. ❖

Contact Corrie at oliveglass@rockisland.com.

Color undulates through this long, flowing lariat

Make

by Nancy Kugel

This necklace may appear daunting, but you'll find your rhythm quickly and string it with ease. Create the color gradation by stringing a pattern, then repeating it in reverse – picture a wave as it crests and retreats. Each strand follows the same pattern, but because seed beads vary in size, subtle color differences appear from strand to strand and add to the effect.

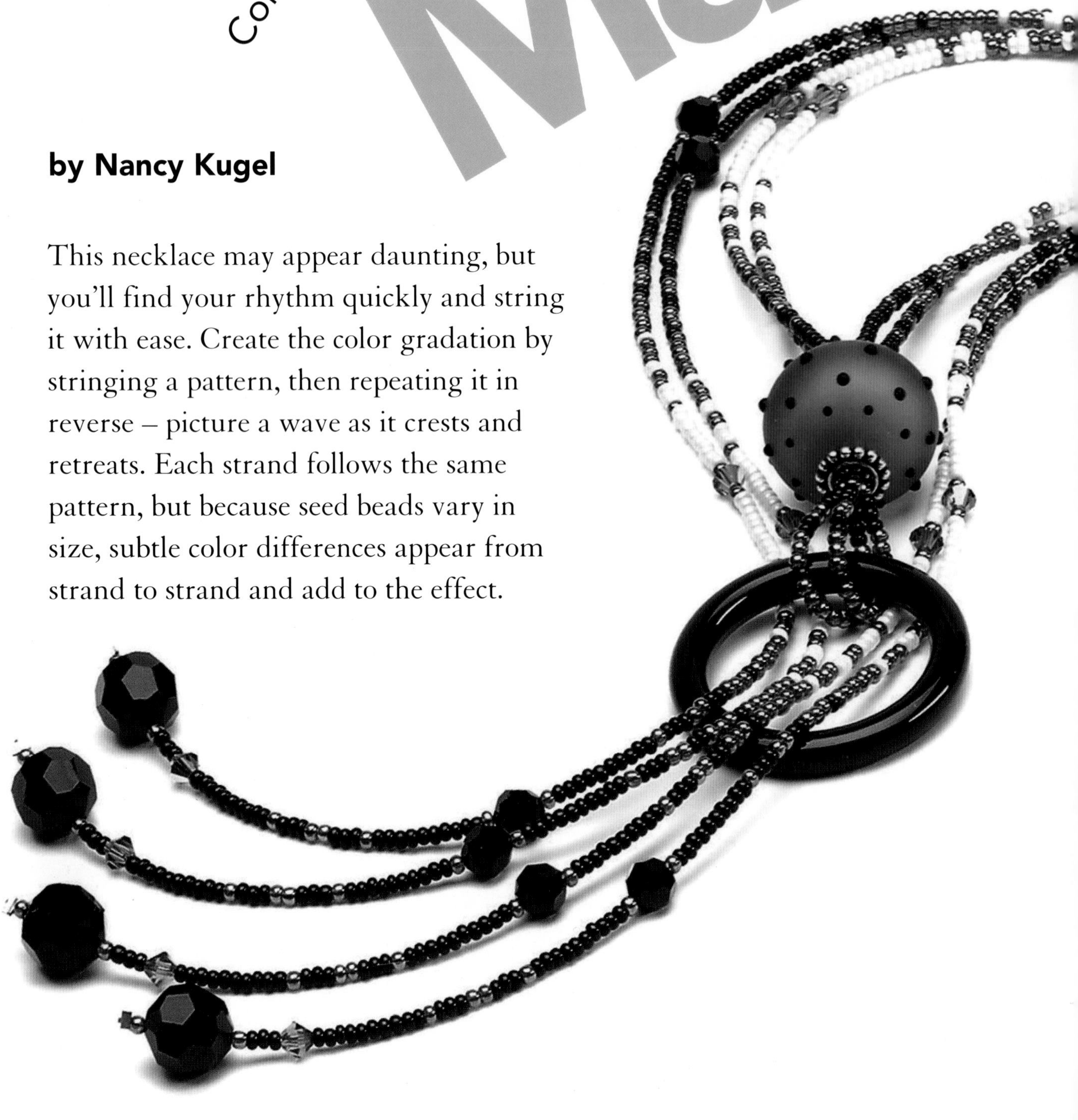

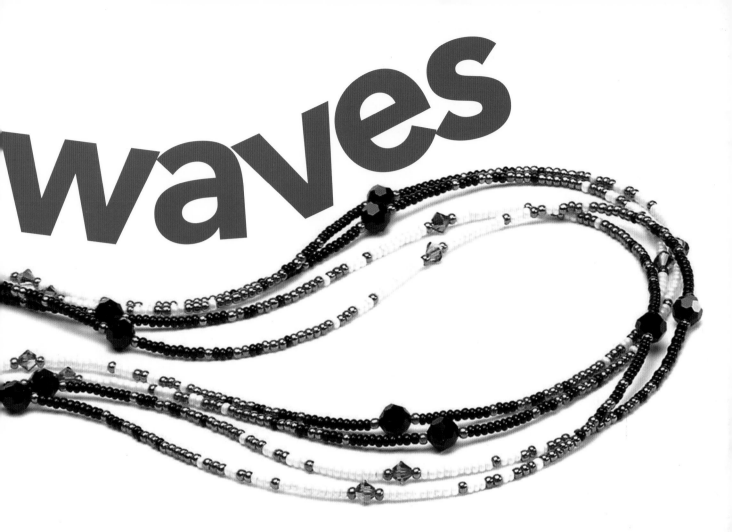

waves

I love the look of black base-metal crimps with this necklace. However, they can be fragile. For more security, use a sterling silver micro crimp at the end of each tassel. – N. K.

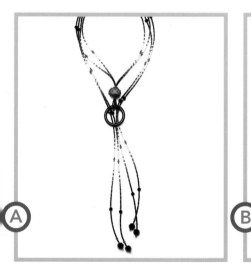

A

1. Wear this necklace with the art bead and ring in the center; the two long ends wrap around your neck and dangle back through the ring. Cut two 60-in. (1.5m) pieces of beading wire.

B

2. String seed beads on each wire in the following pattern: one medium, three dark, two medium, two dark, three medium, one dark, five medium, one dark, three medium, two dark, two medium, three dark, and one medium. Center these beads on the wires.

C

3. Loop the beaded center sections around the ring.

D

4. String all four ends through a spacer, the art bead, and a spacer.

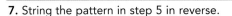

E

5. On one strand, string one medium, ten dark, one medium, three dark, two medium, two dark, three medium, one dark, six medium, one light, three medium, two light, two medium, three light, one medium, ten light, and one medium.

F

6. String a bicone crystal.

G

7. String the pattern in step 5 in reverse.

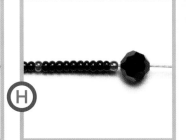

H

8. String a 6mm crystal. Repeat steps 5 through 8 three times.

I

9. String one medium, ten dark, one medium, three dark, two medium, three dark, one medium, ten dark, a bicone, three dark, and one medium.

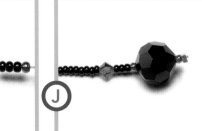

J

10. String a 10mm crystal, a medium seed bead, and a crimp bead. Flatten the crimp bead (Basic Techniques, p. 12) and trim the excess wire.

Repeat steps 5 through 10 on the remaining three strands. ✦

Nancy offers kits for this project. Contact her at EnGee-Kay Designs, LLC, engeekay@sbcglobal.net, or engee-kay.com.

Supply List

- 15 x 20mm "poppy seed" art bead, (Joanne Morash, Blue Iris Designs, 800-431-4747, blueirisdesigns.com)
- 35mm glass ring (Eclectica, 262-641-0910, eclecticabeads.com)
- **24** 4mm bicone crystals
- **16** 6mm round or cube-shaped crystals
- **4** 10mm round or cube-shaped crystals
- **2** flat spacers, 8mm or smaller
- 10g size 11º seed beads, dark color
- 10g size 11º seed beads, medium color
- 10g size 11º seed beads, light color
- flexible beading wire, .014 or .015
- **4** micro crimp beads
- chainnose pliers
- diagonal wire cutters

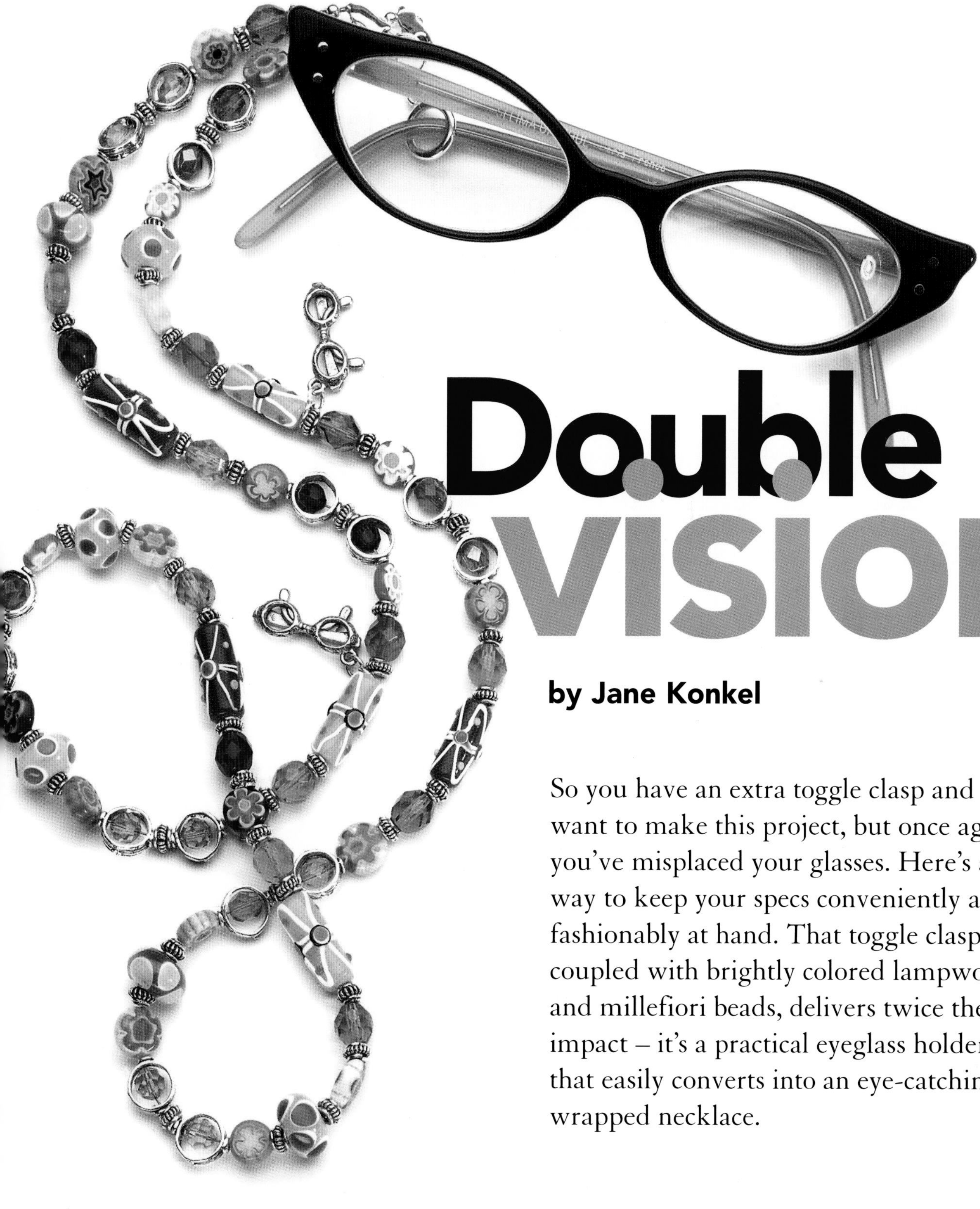

Double
vision

by Jane Konkel

So you have an extra toggle clasp and want to make this project, but once again you've misplaced your glasses. Here's a way to keep your specs conveniently and fashionably at hand. That toggle clasp, coupled with brightly colored lampwork and millefiori beads, delivers twice the impact – it's a practical eyeglass holder that easily converts into an eye-catching wrapped necklace.

A

1. Open the 5mm jump ring (Basic Techniques, p. 12) and string the small loop of the clasp half and the 6mm jump ring. Close the jump ring.

2. Open a 4mm jump ring and attach a charm. Close the jump ring. Repeat with the other charm.

3. Determine the finished length of your eyeglass holder/necklace. (This one is 32 in./81cm.) Add 6 in. (15cm) and cut a piece of beading wire to that length.

B

4. Tape one end of the wire. String beads and spacers as desired, stringing charms approximately 4 in. (10cm) and 24 in. (61cm) from the beginning. Continue stringing beads and spacers until the strand is within 2 in. (5cm) of the desired length.

C

5. Remove the tape. On each end, string a round spacer, crimp bead, round spacer, and lobster claw clasp. Go back through the beads just strung plus a few more. Tighten the wire, check the fit, and add or remove beads if necessary. Crimp the crimp beads (Basic Techniques) and trim the excess wire.

D

6. To wear as an eyeglass holder, attach both lobster claw clasps to the 6mm soldered jump ring and string the temple of your glasses through the large loop of the clasp.

E

7. To wear as a wrapped necklace, cross and wrap each end around to the back of your neck. Attach both lobster clasps to the soldered jump ring. ❖

EDITOR'S TIP
Arrange beads before stringing, positioning complementary beads adjacent to each other.

Supply List

- **18-26** 10mm millefiori disc-shaped beads
- **4-8** 12mm lampwork beads
- **4-8** 9 x 20mm cylinder-shaped beads
- **12-16** 9mm fire-polished Czech crystals
- **12-16** 6mm fire-polished Czech crystals
- **12-16** 11 x 9.5mm round frame beads (Rio Grande, 800-545-6566, riogrande.com)
- **50-60** 4mm flat silver spacers
- **2** charms
- **4** 2mm round silver spacers
- flexible beading wire, .018
- 6mm soldered jump ring
- 5mm jump ring
- **2** 4mm jump rings
- **2** crimp beads
- loop half of toggle clasp
- **2** lobster claw clasps
- chainnose and roundnose pliers or **2** pairs of chainnose pliers
- diagonal wire cutters
- crimping pliers (optional)

Shortcuts

Readers' tips to make your beading life easier

1 removing flattened crimps

When you need to remove a flattened crimp, crimping pliers work far better than chainnose pliers, which tend to slip. Position the notch closest to the tip around the crimp and squeeze gently. The crimp bead will become round and easily slide off the wire.
– Elizabeth Ferris, Carrboro, NC

2 making copies

To help me remember where I purchased beads and findings, I photocopy purchases along with the receipt and the bead store's business card. I can file the information in one place and keep track of prices, both handy for inventory purposes.
– Cecelia M. McDowell, Savannah, GA

3 name and number, please

I have been making name bracelets since I started beading and recently decided to put the birth year on the bracelets. The year adds a special touch to an already personal gift.
– Kathryn Conner, via e-mail

4 gentler pliers

Cover the jaws of your chainnose pliers with painter's tape to prevent the pliers from marring your wire or component. Unlike transparent tape, painter's tape has a little bit of grip to its surface and is easy to remove.
– M. T. Banks, via e-mail

5 snip and tuck

To tuck wire wraps close to the stem of a wrapped loop, use the round notch of your crimping pliers. Position the notch closest to the tip around the trimmed end of the wraps and squeeze gently. You'll have a neat finish without flattening the wraps.
– S. Foster, Newton, MA

Pearls

and shells

Bowtie sensation

From headbands to waistbands and handbags to high heels, bows are topping everything. Create your own stylish statement with this clever beaded choker. Make the bow with crystals, then string pearls on each side. Off center but fashion forward, this bow adds a feminine touch to your favorite outfits.

A faux bow shines on a simple choker

by Christine Griffith

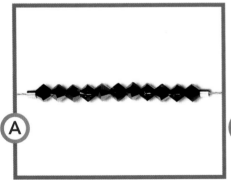

1. Cut a 12-in. (30cm) piece of wire and tape the end. String a crimp bead, 11 bicones, and a crimp bead.

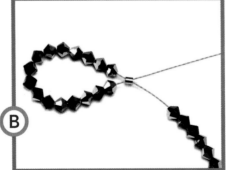

2. String 16 bicones and pass the wire back through the top crimp bead.

3. String 16 bicones and pass the wire back through the crimp bead.

D

4. String 11 bicones and a crimp bead. Tighten the wires and crimp the bead (Basic Techniques, p. 12) at each end. Trim the excess wire. Do not crimp the middle bead.

E

5. Determine the finished length of your necklace. (This one is 15½ in./ 39cm.) Add 6 in. (15cm) and cut a piece of beading wire to that length. String approximately 6 in. of pearls.

Supply List

- **54** 4mm bicone crystals
- 16-in. (41cm) strand 4mm glass pearls
- **4** 3mm spacer beads
- flexible beading wire, .013 or .014 (must pass through the crimp bead five times)
- **5** crimp beads
- lobster claw clasp and split ring or soldered jump ring
- chainnose or crimping pliers
- diagonal wire cutters

F

6. String the bow through the center crimp bead.

G

7. Continue stringing pearls until the necklace is within 1 in. (2.5cm) of the desired length. The bow should be slightly off center.

H

8. On one end of the necklace, string a 3mm spacer, a crimp bead, a 3mm spacer, and the lobster claw clasp. Repeat on the other end with the split ring or soldered jump ring. Tighten the wires.

Check the fit of the necklace and the placement of the bow. Add or remove beads from each end, if necessary. Crimp the crimp beads at each end of the necklace and trim the excess wire. Crimp the bead at the bow's center. ❖

Contact Christine at Beadissimo, (414) 282-2323 or christine@beadissimo.com.

Dynamic design

by Lea Nowicki

Complementary colors individualize an enamel pendant

Selecting beads to coordinate with a pendant should be a fun, creative process – not intimidating or limiting. Bear in mind that beads in contrasting colors keep the focus on the pendant, while matching shades draw attention to the entire necklace. This design is effective in both ways – the individual elements not only complement the centerpiece, but also enrich each other. String crystals throughout the strand for extra flourish and flair.

A

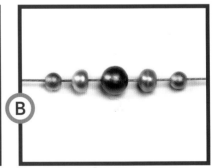

B

lavender necklace • 1. Determine the finished length of your necklace. (The lavender necklace is 18 in./46cm; the blue necklace, 16 in./41cm.) Add 6 in. (15cm) and cut a piece of beading wire to that length. Center the pendant on the wire.

2. On each side of the pendant, string a 3mm pearl and a crystal.

3. On each end, string a brass bead, a 5mm button pearl, a 6mm round pearl, a 5mm pearl, and a brass bead.

SupplyList

both projects
- flexible beading wire, .014 or .015
- chainnose or crimping pliers
- diagonal wire cutters

lavender necklace
- 23 x 27mm enamel pendant with dangles (Rupa Balachandar, rupab.com)
- 16-in. (41cm) strand 5mm freshwater pearls, button
- 16-in. strand 3mm freshwater pearls, rice
- **14** 6mm freshwater pearls, round
- **30** 4mm round matte brass beads (Fire Mountain Gems, 800-355-2137, firemountaingems.com)
- **28** 4mm bicone crystals

- **2** crimp beads
- lobster claw clasp and 6mm split ring

blue necklace
- 10 x 15mm enamel pendant with dangles (Rupa Balachandar)
- 16-in. strand 5mm freshwater pearls, potato
- 16-in. strand 2mm freshwater pearls, rice
- **12** 6mm round beads, lapis lazuli
- **26** 3.2mm round matte brass beads (Fire Mountain Gems)
- **24** 4mm bicone crystals
- **2** crimp beads
- lobster claw clasp and 6mm split ring

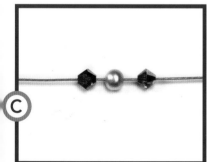

4. On each end, string a crystal, a 3mm rice pearl, and a crystal. Repeat steps 3 and 4 on each end until the necklace is within 1 in. (2.5cm) of the desired length.

5. On one end, string a brass bead, a crimp bead, a brass bead, and the clasp. Go back through the last three beads and tighten the wire. Repeat on the other end, substituting a split ring for the clasp. Check the fit, and add or remove beads from each end if necessary. Crimp the crimp beads (Basic Techniques, p. 12) and trim the excess wire.

blue necklace • 1. Follow step 1 of the lavender necklace.

2. On each side of the pendant, string a rice pearl and a crystal.

3. On each end, string a brass bead, a potato-shaped pearl, a round lapis lazuli, a potato pearl, and a brass bead.

4. On each end, string a crystal, a rice pearl, and a crystal. Repeat steps 3 and 4 on each end until the necklace is within 1 in. of the desired length.

5. Follow step 5 of the lavender necklace to finish the blue necklace. ✤

Contact Lea in care of BeadStyle.

by Beth Stone

Variations
on a theme

Design two bracelets from common denominators: pearls and silver

Pearls and silver together speak sophistication. String the small bracelet when subtlety suits the occasion. Try the larger bracelet for a bolder impact. Both options will give you classic results.

large bracelet • 1. Determine the finished length of your bracelet, add 5 in. (13cm), and cut a piece of beading wire to that length. Center an alternating pattern of three pearls and two spacers on the wire.

2. On one end, string a 10mm silver bead, a pearl, spacer, pearl, spacer, pearl, and a 10mm silver bead, alternating the silver bead shapes.
  On the other end, string the pattern in reverse.

3. On each end, string an alternating pattern of pearls and spacers until the bracelet is within 1 in. (2.5cm) of the desired length. End with a pearl.

4. On one end, string a 5mm bead cap or spacer, round spacer, crimp bead, round spacer, and half the clasp. Go back through the beads just strung and tighten the wire. Repeat on the other end. Check the fit, and add or remove beads from each end if necessary. Crimp the crimp beads (Basic Techniques, p. 12) and trim the excess wire.

SupplyList

both projects
- flexible beading wire, .014 or .015
- chainnose or crimping pliers
- diagonal wire cutters

large bracelet
- **10–16** 8mm or larger potato pearls
- **4** 10mm or larger silver beads, in two shapes
- **6–12** 3-4mm flat spacers
- **2** 5mm bead caps or spacers
- **4** 3mm round spacers
- **2** crimp beads
- clasp

small bracelet
- **24–30** 3mm rice pearls
- **8** 6-9mm silver beads, in two shapes
- **4** 3mm round spacers
- **2** crimp beads
- clasp

small bracelet • 1. Determine the finished length of your bracelet, add 5 in., and cut a piece of beading wire to that length. String a silver bead and three pearls. Repeat seven or eight times, alternating large bead shapes. End with a silver bead.

2. String three or more pearls on each end, until the bracelet is within 1 in. of the desired length.

EDITOR'S TIP
Use a toggle or box clasp that mimics the shape of one of the silver beads.

3. On one end, string a round spacer, crimp bead, round spacer, and half the clasp. Go back through the beads just strung and tighten the wire. Repeat on the other end. Check the fit, and add or remove beads from each end, if necessary. Crimp the crimp beads and trim the excess wire. ✤

Contact Beth at (248) 855-9358 or bnshdl@msn.com.

Create a clever
two-tiered necklace
and complementary
earrings

by Rupa Balachandar

Chain continues to
appear in unexpected
ways. Here, chain pairs
with a beaded strand in an
interesting dichotomy —
luminous coin pearls hang
from delicate chain, then reappear
within the shorter beaded strand.
Accompanied by uncomplicated
earrings, this design invites a second look.

Double
take

A

B

necklace • 1. Determine the finished length of your necklace. (The chain is 18 in./46cm; the beaded strand, 17 in./43cm.) Add 6 in. (15cm) and cut a piece of beading wire to that length. Cut a piece of chain to the desired length.

String a chip on a head pin. Make a plain loop (Basic Techniques, p. 12) above the chip. Make a second dangle.

2. String a flat spacer, a coin pearl, and a flat spacer on an eye pin. Make a wrapped loop (Basic Techniques) above the top spacer, perpendicular to the bottom loop. Make a second pearl component.

C

D

3. Open the plain loop on a pearl component and string the two chip dangles. Close the loop. Open the plain loop of the second pearl component and string the wrapped loop of the first pearl component. Close the loop. Open a jump ring (Basic Techniques) and attach the entire dangle. Close the jump ring. Center the dangle on the chain.

4. Center a flat spacer, a pearl, and a flat spacer on the beading wire.

EDITOR'S TIP

To make eye pins, trim the head from a head pin and make a plain loop at one end, or make a plain loop on the end of a 2-in. (5cm) piece of 22-gauge wire.

Contact Rupa at rupa@rupab.com or visit her website, rupab.com.

Supply List

necklace
- 16-in. (41cm) strand 6-8mm gemstone chips or keshi pearls
- **7** 12mm coin pearls, round or rectangular
- **18** 5mm flat spacers
- **2** 1½-in. (3.8cm) eye pins
- **2** 1½-in. head pins
- **5** 4mm jump rings
- **4** 3mm round spacer beads
- 20 in. (51cm) 1.6mm long-and-short chain
- flexible beading wire, .014 or .015
- **2** crimp beads
- two-strand box clasp with attached jump rings
- chainnose and roundnose pliers
- diagonal wire cutters
- crimping pliers (optional)

earrings
- **2** 6-8mm gemstone chips or keshi pearls
- **2** 12mm coin pearls, round or rectangular
- **2** 5mm flat spacers
- **2** 1½-in. eye pins
- **2** 1½-in. head pins
- pair of earring wires
- chainnose and roundnose pliers
- diagonal wire cutters

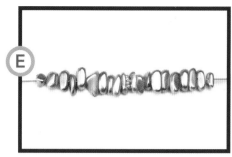

E

5. On each end, string ten chips, a spacer, and ten chips.

6. Repeat steps 4 and 5 once more, then step 4 again, on each end. String chips until the necklace is within 1 in. (2.5cm) of the desired length.

F

7. Open four jump rings. Attach one to each one of the clasp's jump rings. Close the jump rings. On each end of the beaded strand, string a round spacer, a crimp bead, a round spacer, and jump rings just attached to the clasp. Go back through the beads just strung plus one or two more and tighten the wire. Check the fit, and add or remove beads from each end, if necessary. Crimp the crimp beads (Basic Techniques) and trim the excess wire. Open the remaining jump rings and attach each end link of chain. Close the jump rings. If necessary, trim the chain.

A

earrings • 1. String a chip on a head pin. Make a plain loop above the chip.

B

2. String a flat spacer and a coin pearl on an eye pin. Make a wrapped loop above the pearl.

C

3. Open the plain loop of the pearl component and attach the dangle. Close the loop. Open an earring wire and attach the wrapped loop. Close the earring wire. Make a second earring to match the first. ❖

Alluring

Combine freshwater pearls with silver accents to create a triple-strand bracelet

by Gretta Van Someren

More accessible than ever, freshwater pearls are tantalizing because they add texture and luster to your finished piece. String your strands solely of pearls or combine them inventively with bold-colored crystals and silver spacers. A stunning three-strand bracelet results.

pearls

1. Determine the finished length of your bracelet, add 5 in. (13cm), and cut three pieces of beading wire to that length. On the top and bottom strands, string the same pattern of flat spacers, pearls, and 2mm and 4mm rounds. On the middle strand, string a pattern of pearls, flat spacers, and 2mm rounds. Center the beads on each wire. Each beaded section should measure 1½ in. (3.8cm) or less.

2. On each end of each strand, string a 2mm round, a bicone crystal, a 2mm round, and the corresponding hole of a spacer bar.

3. On each end of each strand, string a pattern of 2mm rounds, pearls, and spacer tubes. End with a 3mm round.

Supply List

- **36–40** 4mm freshwater round pearls
- **7** 4mm bicone crystals
- **2** 4 x 15mm 3-hole spacer bars
- **6** 5 x 8mm cones
- **6** 2 x 4mm spacer tubes
- **3** x 5mm bead cap
- **14–16** 4mm flat spacers
- **36** or more 2mm and 4mm round spacer beads
- **6** 3mm round spacer beads
- **1½-in.** (3.8cm) head pin
- **2** 5 x 12mm or 6 x 19mm three-to-one connector bars
- **1** in. (2.5cm) open-link chain, 4mm
- **3** 4mm jump rings
- flexible beading wire, .014 or .015
- **6** crimp beads
- **2¼** in. (5.7cm) or more French bullion or **6** 2mm round spacer beads
- hook clasp
- chainnose and roundnose pliers
- diagonal wire cutters

4. On each end of each wire strand, string a cone, 2mm round, crimp bead, and the corresponding loop of a connector bar. Go back through the beads just strung, check the fit, and add or remove an equal number of beads from each end, if necessary. If desired, cut six ⅜-in. (1cm) lengths of French bullion. String the bullion – a tube of coiled wire – after the crimp bead on each wire, or replace the bullion with a second 2mm round. Tighten the wires and crimp the crimp beads (Basic Techniques, p. 12). Trim the excess wire.

5. To make the chain extender, string a crystal, a bead cap, and a pearl on a head pin. Make the first half of a wrapped loop (Basic Techniques) above the pearl. Attach it to the end link of a 1-in. (2.5cm) section of chain and complete the wraps.

EDITOR'S TIP

Pearl sizes vary within individual strands. To ensure a proper fit, use pearls of consistent size. This will keep the spacer bars straight and help your bracelet lay flat.

6. Open a jump ring (Basic Techniques). String a connector bar's end loop and the extender chain's end link. Close the jump ring. Attach a hook clasp to the remaining connector bar's loop using two jump rings. ❖

Contact Gretta at (920) 954-0879 or gretta@pizzazzcreations.com.

INFORMATION, PLEASE...

For a polished, professional-looking finish, try French wire (bullion). After you have checked the bracelet's fit, cut the tube of coiled wire to length and thread it over beading wire in place of a final round spacer bead. It is available in both precious and plated metals and in widths ranging from .8-2.5mm. Beginning beaders may find thicker bullion less likely to crush and uncoil, and therefore, easier to use.

Pendant panache

String a stylish
substitute for
a store-bought
drop

by Beth Stone

By employing a little creativity, you can quickly arrange a few
loose beads into a fabulous focal point. This easy option lets you keep
stringing, even when you don't have a purchased pendant on hand.
Let the dangles stand alone – framed with sparkling seed beads –
or continue stringing beads around the necklace for a fuller look.

vertical drop necklace • 1. Determine the finished length of your necklace. (This one is 16 in./41cm with a 1½-in./ 3.8cm drop.) Add 10 in. (25cm) and cut a piece of beading wire to that length.

String the focal bead onto a head pin. If its hole is too large for the head pin, string a spacer on each end. Make a wrapped loop (Basic Techniques, p. 12) above the top bead.

2. Center the bead on the wire. On each side, string a seed bead, a pearl, a seed bead, and a pearl.

3. Pass each end through a 6mm spacer in opposite directions and pull the wires to form a loop.

4. On each end, string a seed bead, a pearl, a seed bead, and a pearl. Pass each end through a 6mm spacer in opposite directions and pull the wires to form a loop.

5. String alternating colors of seed beads on each end until you are within 1 in. (2.5cm) of the desired length.

6. String a 3mm round spacer, a crimp bead, a spacer, and a flower spacer or jump ring. Go back through the last beads strung and tighten the wire. Repeat on the other end, substituting a lobster claw clasp for the flower spacer or jump ring. Check the fit and add or remove an equal number of beads from each end, if necessary. Crimp the crimp beads (Basic Techniques) and trim the excess wire.

SupplyList

vertical drop necklace
- 8-10mm round focal bead
- **8** 6mm round pearls
- **2** 6mm oval spacers
- 2g faceted size 11º seed beads, two colors
- **2** 4mm flat spacer beads (optional)
- **4** 3mm round spacer beads
- 1½-in. (3.8cm) head pin
- flexible beading wire, .014 or .015
- **2** crimp beads
- lobster claw clasp
- 10mm open petal flower spacer or soldered jump ring
- chainnose and roundnose pliers
- diagonal wire cutters
- crimping pliers (optional)

round drop necklace
- **10** 6mm round pearls, **5** each of two colors
- **9** 3-5mm spacers, assorted shapes
- 6mm spacer
- 2g faceted size 11º seed beads, two colors
- **4** 3mm round spacer beads
- flexible beading wire, .014 or .015
- **2** crimp beads
- lobster claw clasp
- 10mm open petal flower spacer or soldered jump ring
- chainnose or d
- diagonal wire

round drop necklace • 1. Determine the finished length of your necklace. (This one is 16 in. with a 1½-in. drop). Add 10 in. and cut a piece of beading wire to that length. String pearls and 5mm spacers, alternating the colors of the pearls. Center the beads on the wire.

2. Pass each end through a 6mm spacer in opposite directions and pull the wires to form a loop. Follow steps 5 and 6 of the vertical drop necklace to finish. ❖

Contact Beth at b
(248) 855-9358.

Net results

Knot pearls in tulle for an up-to-date, two-strand necklace

by Paulette Biedenbender

A

1. Determine the finished length of your necklace (the longer strand in this necklace is 18 in./46cm), double that measurement, and add 6 in. (15cm). Cut two strips of tulle to that length with a width 3½ times wider than the bead's diameter. Set one length aside.

2. Fold the tulle into thirds, with each edge meeting the opposite fold.

B

3. Keeping the tulle folded, tie an overhand knot (Basic Techniques, p. 12) 6 in. from one end.

C

4. To make the inner strand, insert a 6mm bead under one of the folds and slide the bead against the knot.

SupplyList

- 21-in. (53cm) strand 6mm round Swarovski pearls
- 21-in. strand 10mm round shell pearls
- 1½ yds. (1.37m) tulle
- button with shank
- scissors

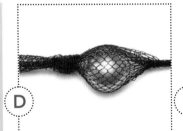

D

5. Overlap the opposite fold of tulle over the bead, and twist in the same direction as the top edge.

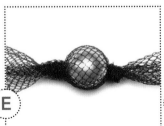

E

6. Tie a loose overhand knot, keeping the tulle twisted by pinching the fabric near the bead. Slide the knot against the bead and tighten.

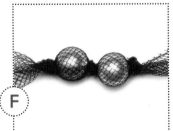

F

7. Repeat steps 4 through 6. Check the length as you go until you are 1¼ in. (3.1cm) from the desired length.

8. To complete the outer strand, use 10mm rounds or a pattern of 10mm and 6mm rounds. Repeat steps 2 through 7 until you are 1 in. (2.5cm) from the desired length.

Contact Paulette in care of BeadStyle.

Here's a new twist on the multistrand pearl necklace: Transform round glass or shell pearls and off-the-bolt tulle into a lavish necklace without a lavish price. Everyday materials will produce extraordinary results.

9. Match up the last knot on each strand and make a surgeon's knot (Basic Techniques) ½ in. (1.3cm) from the knots. Thread one strand of the tulle through the button's shank.

10. Tie a surgeon's knot on the other side of the shank, and trim the excess tulle ½ to 1 in. from the knot.

11. At the other end of the necklace, make a surgeon's knot ½ in. from the beads. Tie a second surgeon's knot, making a loop that will fit around the button. Trim the excess tulle ½ to 1 in. from the knot. ✣

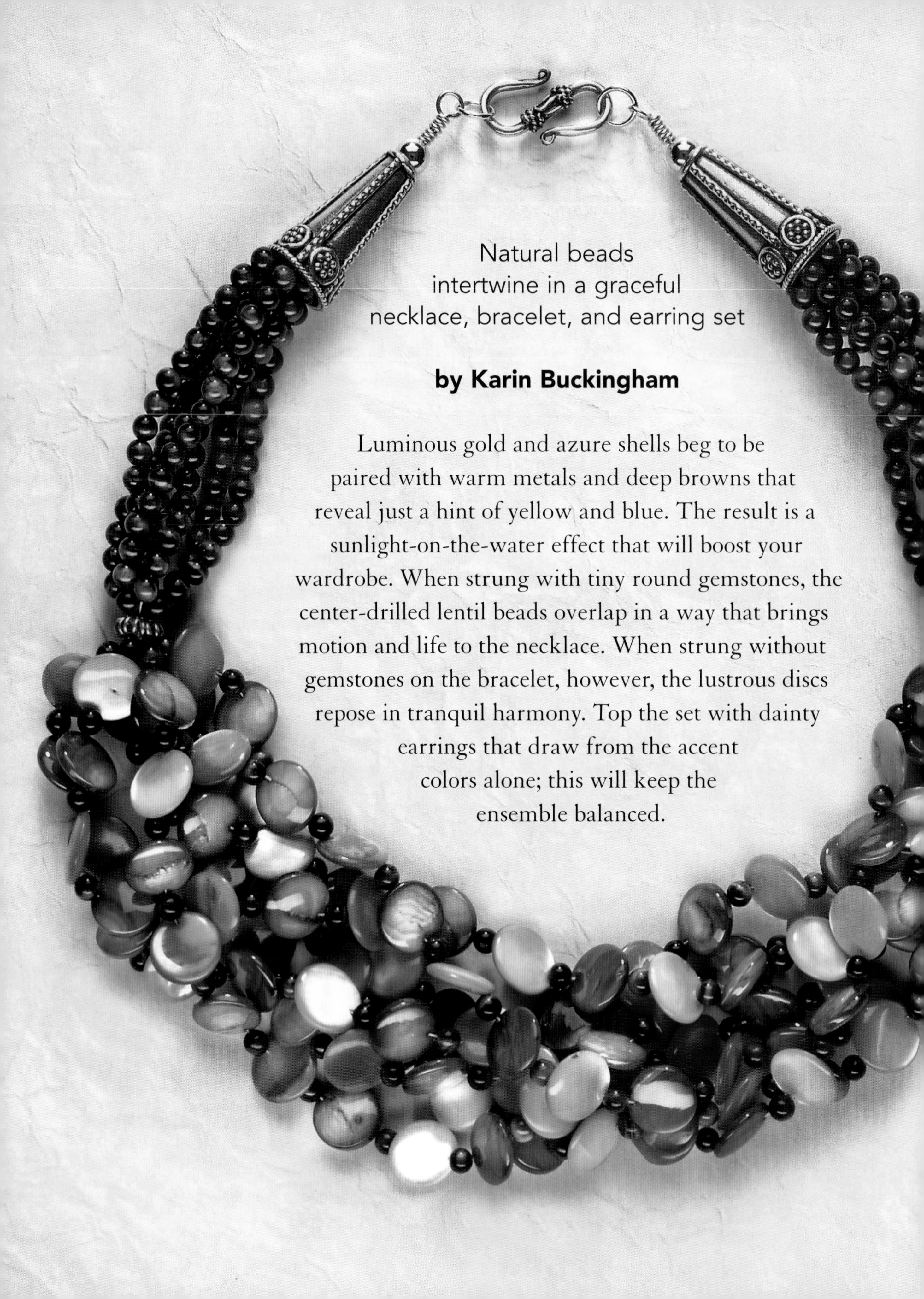

Natural beads
intertwine in a graceful
necklace, bracelet, and earring set

by Karin Buckingham

Luminous gold and azure shells beg to be
paired with warm metals and deep browns that
reveal just a hint of yellow and blue. The result is a
sunlight-on-the-water effect that will boost your
wardrobe. When strung with tiny round gemstones, the
center-drilled lentil beads overlap in a way that brings
motion and life to the necklace. When strung without
gemstones on the bracelet, however, the lustrous discs
repose in tranquil harmony. Top the set with dainty
earrings that draw from the accent
colors alone; this will keep the
ensemble balanced.

Shell harmony

necklace • **1.** Determine the finished length of your necklace. (This one is 18 in./46cm.) Add 6 in. (15cm) and cut seven pieces of beading wire to that length. String a gemstone, a light lentil, a gemstone, and a dark lentil. Repeat until the beaded strand is 8½ in. (21.6cm) long, ending with a gemstone. Repeat on the other strands, beginning some with light lentils and some with dark lentils.

2. On each end, string a spacer over all seven wires.

3. String 15 gemstones on each strand. Repeat on the other end.

4. Check the fit, allowing approximately 3 in. (7.6cm) for finishing. Add or remove gemstones, if necessary.

5. Cut a 3-in. (7.6cm) piece of 20-gauge wire. Make a wrapped loop (Basic Techniques, p. 12) at one end.

E

F

G

6. String a seed bead, a crimp bead, a seed bead, and the wire loop. Go back through the beads just strung. Repeat with each strand.

7. Repeat steps 5 and 6 on the other end. Tighten the wires and crimp the crimp beads (Basic Techniques). Trim the excess wire.

8. Slide a cone and a 5mm bead on the wire. Make the first half of a wrapped loop above the bead, and slide a jump ring on the loop. Complete the wraps. Repeat on the other end.

9. Attach the clasp to one jump ring.

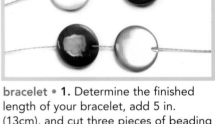

A

bracelet • 1. Determine the finished length of your bracelet, add 5 in. (13cm), and cut three pieces of beading wire to that length. String lentils, alternating colors, until the beaded portion of each strand is within 1 in. (2.5cm) of the desired length.

B

2. String two seed beads, a crimp bead, two seed beads, and the corresponding loop on half the clasp. Go back through the beads just strung. Repeat on the other end. Tighten the wires, check the fit, and add or remove beads, if necessary. Crimp the crimp beads and trim the excess wire.

SupplyList

necklace
- **2** 15-in. (38cm) strands 12mm lentils, gold lip shell (Fire Mountain Gems, 800-355-2137 firemountaingems.com)
- **2** 16-in. strands 11mm lentils, blue shell (Fire Mountain Gems)
- **4** 16-in. (41cm) strands 4mm round gemstones, yellow-blue tigereye (Fire Mountain Gems)
- **2** 7mm large-hole spacer discs
- **2** 5mm round beads
- 1g size 11º seed beads
- **2** 12 x 25mm cones
- 6 in. (15cm) 20-gauge wire
- flexible beading wire, .014 or .015
- **14** crimp beads
- S-hook clasp and **2** soldered jump rings
- chainnose and roundnose pliers
- diagonal wire cutters
- crimping pliers (optional)

bracelet
- 12mm lentils, gold lip shell, leftover from necklace
- 11mm lentils, blue shell, leftover from necklace
- size 11º seed beads, left over from necklace
- flexible beading wire, .014 or .015
- **6** crimp beads
- 3-strand clasp
- chainnose or crimping pliers
- diagonal wire cutters

earrings
- **6** 4mm round gemstones, yellow-blue tigereye
- **10** 3mm round beads
- **2** 7 x 10mm cones
- **8** 2-in. (5cm) head pins
- pair of earring wires
- chainnose and roundnose pliers
- diagonal wire cutters

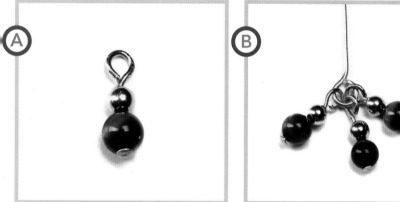

earrings • 1. String a gemstone and a 3mm round on a head pin. Make a plain loop (Basic Techniques) above the top bead. Make a total of three bead units.

2. Trim the head from a head pin and make a plain loop at the end. Open the loop, attach the gemstone dangles, and close the loop.

3. String a 3mm bead, a cone, and a 3mm bead on the head pin.

4. Make a wrapped loop above the top bead. Open the loop of an earring wire and attach the dangle. Close the loop. Make a second earring to match the first. ❖

Contact Karin in care of BeadStyle.

73

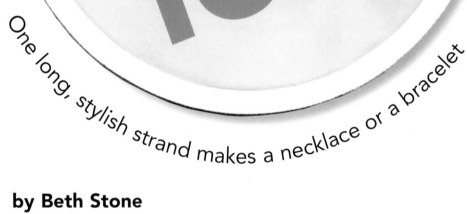

2.1 for

One long, stylish strand makes a necklace or a bracelet

by Beth Stone

Wrapped eight times around your wrist or draped three times around your neck, one effort yields two results: a strand of pearls that adds up to a versatile accessory. Because the pattern is random and the length is flexible, it's easy to use materials left over from other projects. Or, purchase multicolored strands of pearls to get the most variety for your money.

necklace/bracelet • 1. Determine the finished length of your combination necklace/bracelet by loosely measuring your wrist and multiplying the result by the number of wraps you desire. (This project uses eight.) Divide this measurement by three to check your necklace strand length. (These strands are about 17 in./4.3cm each.) Add 6 in. (1.5cm) for finishing and cut a piece of flexible beading wire to that length.

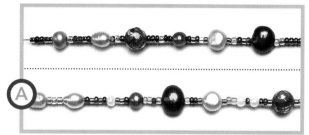

2. String assorted seed beads and pearls. This project uses six pearl shapes spaced with up to five seed beads. Use three complementary and two accent seed bead colors.

3. String a 3mm round bead, a crimp bead, a round, and the clasp. Go back through the beads just strung and tighten the wire. Repeat on the other side, substituting a split ring for the clasp. Check the length and add or remove beads if necessary (the bracelet fit is more critical than the necklace fit). Crimp the crimp beads (Basic Techniques, p. 12) and trim the excess wire.

BONUS BUY!

Make matching earrings from the same stash

A

earrings • 1. String a variety of seed beads and pearls on six head pins. Make the first half of a wrapped loop (Basic Techniques) above each top bead.

B

2. Cut a ½-in. (1.3cm) length of chain. String a dangle through the bottom link and complete the wraps.

C

3. Repeat with two more dangles.

D

4. Open the loop on an earring wire and slide the top chain link onto the loop. Close the loop. Repeat steps 2 through 4 to make a second earring. ✤

Contact Beth at bnshdl@msn.com or (248) 855-9358.

SupplyList

necklace/bracelet
- **125-140** 3-6mm freshwater pearls, assorted shapes and colors
- 3g size 11º seed beads in five colors
- **4** 3mm round spacer beads
- flexible beading wire, .014 or .015
- **2** crimp beads
- lobster claw clasp and split ring
- chainnose or crimping pliers
- diagonal wire cutters

earrings
- pearls left over from necklace
- seed beads left over from necklace
- **6** 2-in. (5.1cm) head pins
- 1 in. (2.5cm) 2.8mm cable chain
- pair of earring wires
- chainnose and roundnose pliers
- diagonal wire cutters

Practical indulgence

Design two pearl necklaces from the same set of beads • **by Beth Stone**

Long, lustrous strands of pearls are tempting to most bead shoppers. But if you question the practicality of buying several strands for a single project, you can solve this dilemma by creating two very different necklaces with the same materials. In this way, you can happily indulge your creativity while feeling satisfied with your bead purchases.

SupplyList

dangle necklace
- **15** 10mm oval pearls, **10** light colored and **5** dark colored
- **30** 2mm flat spacers
- **3g** size 11º seed beads in two colors
- **5** 1½-in. (3.8cm) head pins
- **4** 3mm round beads
- flexible beading wire, .014 or .015
- **2** crimp beads
- lobster claw clasp and split ring or open-petal flower spacer
- chainnose and roundnose pliers

teardrop necklace
- **9** 10mm oval pearls
- **48** 4 x 5mm teardrop pearls
- **18** 6mm flat spacers
- **3g** size 11º seed beads in two colors
- **4** 3mm round beads
- flexible beading wire, .014 or .015
- **2** crimp beads
- lobster claw clasp and split ring or open-petal flower spacer
- chainnose or crimping pliers
- diagonal wire cutters

- diagonal wire cutters
- crimping pliers (optional)

A

B

C

dangle necklace • 1. String a dark pearl on a head pin and make a wrapped loop (Basic Techniques, p. 12). Make a total of five dangles.

2. Determine the finished length of your necklace. (This one is 16 in./41cm.) Add 6 in. (15cm) and cut a piece of flexible beading wire to that length.

3. String a flat spacer, a dangle, and a flat spacer on the wire.

4. On each end, string seven seed beads (alternating colors), a flat spacer, a light pearl, a flat spacer, and seven seed beads. Repeat the patterns in steps 3 and 4 twice on each end.

D

E

5. String eight seed beads on each end, then a spacer, a pearl, and a spacer. String 21 seed beads, a flat spacer, a pearl, and a flat spacer on each end. String seed beads on each end until the necklace is within 1 in. (2.5cm) of the desired length.

6. String a round bead, a crimp bead, a round, and the clasp. Go back through the beads just strung and a few more. Repeat on the other end with a split ring or flower spacer. Tighten the wires and check the fit. Add or remove beads from each end, if necessary. Crimp the crimp beads (Basic Techniques) and trim the excess wire.

A

B

teardrop necklace • 1. Determine the finished length of your necklace. (This one is 16 in.) Add 6 in. and cut a piece of flexible beading wire to that length.

2. Center three teardrop pearls, a 6mm spacer, an oval pearl, a spacer, and three teardrops on the wire.

3. On each end, string 11 seed beads, alternating colors. Repeat the patterns in steps 2 and 3 three times on each end.

C

D

4. String three teardrops, a spacer, an oval, and a spacer.

5. Attach the clasp as in step 6 of the dangle necklace. ❖

Contact Beth at (248) 855-9358 or bnshdl@msn.com.

Cluster pearls and crystals for an embellished cuff

Off the cuff

by Lynne Dixon-Speller

An understated blouse speaks volumes when the cuffs are adorned with pearl-clustered links. A lonely lapel springs to life with one bauble in its buttonhole. This pair of cuff links is a versatile addition to your jewelry wardrobe, and might be all you need to move your classic suit from drab to fab.

A

1. String nine head pins with a 6mm pearl, and nine head pins with a crystal and a 4mm pearl. Make a wrapped loop (Basic Techniques, p. 12) on each head pin above the top bead.

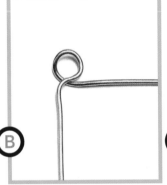

B

2. Cut an 8-in. (20cm) piece of wire and make the first half of a wrapped loop 1½ in. (3.8cm) from one end. Make your loop 3mm-4mm in diameter to accommodate all the pearl units.

C

3. Slide the pearl units onto the loop, alternating styles. Complete one wrap and trim the excess wire.

D

4. Slide a flat bead and a spacer onto the wire.

E

5. Bend the wire at a right angle ½ in. (1.3cm) from the spacer. (Adjust the length for a longer or shorter cuff link.)

F

6. Make the first half of a wrapped loop and slide on a toggle end.

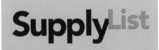

G

7. Complete the wraps down the length of the wire until flush with the spacer. Trim the excess wire. Make a second cuff link to match the first. ❖

Contact Lynne in care of BeadStyle.

SupplyList

- 16-in. (.41m) strand 6mm rice-shaped freshwater pearls
- 16-in. strand 4mm rice-shaped freshwater pearls
- 18 4mm bicone crystals
- 2 20mm square center-drilled mother-of-pearl flat beads (Eclectica, 262-641-0910)
- 2 6mm flat spacers
- 36 1½-in. (38mm) decorative head pins
- 2 toggle bars
- 16 in. wire, 20 gauge
- chainnose and roundnose pliers
- diagonal wire cutters

Shortcuts

Readers' tips to make your beading life easier

1 smart storage

Store tiny essentials such as crimp beads and jump rings in 35mm-film canisters. With a permanent marker, label each canister with its contents. To make findings more accessible, arrange the canisters you use most in the front of a tray or box.
– Veronica Miller, Pittsburgh, PA

2 sorting beads

To sort beads of various sizes, position a colander over a large bowl and pour the beads into it. The smallest beads will fall through the colander's holes. This method works especially well to separate seed beads from larger beads.
– Judy Danielson, Marble Falls, TX

3 easy embellishment

Beaded ribbons make easy, pretty decorations on gift boxes or bags. Thread a few leftover beads on a piece of organza or satin ribbon and tie a knot at each end. When wrapping a large box, tie a ribbon around it first, then thread beads, knot the ends, and trim the excess ribbon.
– L. D. Fisher, Oakland, CA

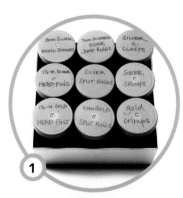

4 beading tray

A metal cookie sheet or large baking pan can double as a portable tray to hold your projects and tools. Simply line the pan with a dish towel, and your loose beads and findings will stay put. When you're done with a project, shake out the towel over a trash can to prevent wire clippings and broken beads from becoming embedded in your work space.
– Jane Posten-Buckley, New York, NY

5 checking colorfastness

To determine if gemstone beads have been dyed, dip them in warm water. If the water changes color, the beads have been dyed. You also can clean gemstones with warm water. Just add a little mild dishwashing liquid and rinse.
– N. Hunter, via e-mail

Metal

and chain

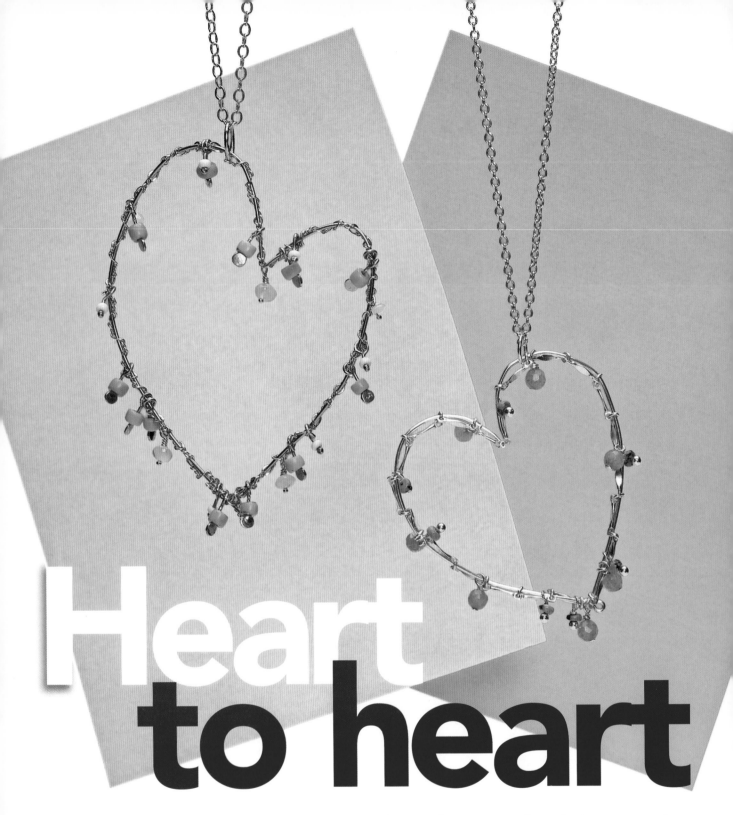

Heart to heart

Sculpt a chain-wrapped heart pendant for a lovely necklace

by Brenda Schweder

Show your openhearted nature with a chain-wrapped, embellished wire pendant necklace. First, make a basic shape with gold-filled or sterling wire and chain. Next, attach several dainty beads around the perimeter. Try different pendant shapes (a moon or a star?) and necklace lengths, then layer randomly. Everyone will respect your heartfelt intentions.

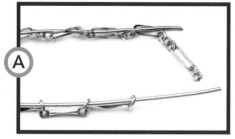

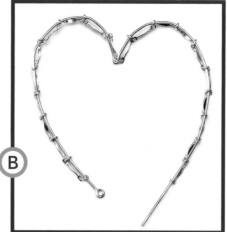

1. Determine the finished size of your pendant. (The gold heart is approximately 3 in./7.6cm; the silver, 2 in./5cm.) Multiply the number by four and cut a piece of 20-gauge wire to that length.

Cut a piece of chain to that length. If using chain with long and short links, string the wire through each long link, twisting the short links around the wire. If using bar-and-link chain, string the wire through each link.

2. Carefully bend the chain-wrapped wire in half. With your fingers, shape each half to form a heart. At one end, make a small plain loop (Basic Techniques, p. 12) with the wire.

SupplyList

85

- 6-14 in. (15-36cm) 20-gauge wire, gold-filled or sterling silver, half-hard
- 6-14 in. chain with long and short links or bar-and-link style
- 17-25 in. (43-64cm) cable chain
- 10–25 2-4mm accent beads
- 10–25 1-in. (2.5cm) head pins, plain and/or decorative
- 6-8mm jump ring
- 2 4mm jump rings
- lobster claw clasp and soldered jump ring
- chainnose and roundnose pliers
- diagonal wire cutters

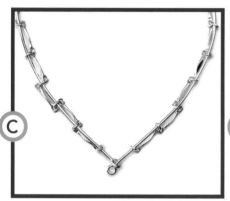

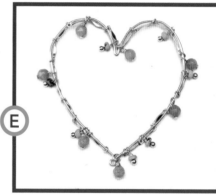

3. String the other end of the wire through the plain loop. Make a plain loop and trim the excess wire and chain.

4. String a bead on a head pin and make a plain loop or the first half of a wrapped loop (Basic Techniques). Make dangles to attach to the wire form as desired, using plain or decorative head pins, or both.

5. Open the loop on a dangle and attach it to the wire form where desired. Close the loop (or complete the wraps). You can attach dangles to the chain, the wire, or both. Attach the remaining dangles.

> **EDITOR'S TIP**
> Select a chain with links of varying sizes; it will wrap more easily around the wire form.

Brenda offers kits for this project. Contact her at Miss Cellany Jewelry Kits, b@brendaschweder.com, or visit brendaschweder.com.

6. Open a 6-8mm jump ring. Link it to the form between the chain and the wire. Determine the finished length of your necklace. (Both necklaces are 20 in./51cm.) Cut a piece of chain to that length and string the pendant.

7. Open a 4mm jump ring (Basic Techniques). String an end link of chain and the clasp. Close the jump ring. Check the fit, and trim the chain's other end if necessary.

Open a 4mm jump ring. String the remaining end link and a soldered jump ring. Close the jump ring. ❧

Chain
change
chain

by Margot Potter

Combine an interchangeable dangle with chain for a modern necklace

The key to this contemporary necklace is to keep things streamlined. Three graduated lengths of chain dangle from the removable center toggle, while a single chain makes for simple, edgy earrings. Create dangles in a variety of colors for maximum versatility.

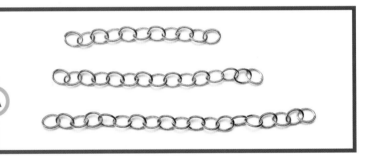

A

necklace • 1. Determine the finished length of your necklace. (This one is 19 in./48cm with a 3-in./7.6cm dangle.) Cut six lengths of chain: three to the desired necklace length, one 2½ in. (6.4cm) long, one 2 in. (5cm) long, and one 1⅝ in. (4cm) long.

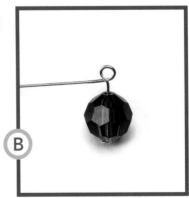

B

2. To make the bead units, string a bead on each of three head pins. Make the first half of a wrapped loop (Basic Techniques, p. 12) above each bead.

C

3. Attach a bead unit to each of the three shortest chain segments. Complete the wraps.

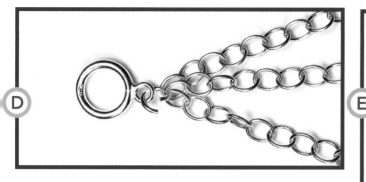

D

4. Open a jump ring (Basic Techniques). String each dangle's end link and the small loop of the extra half of the toggle clasp. Close the jump ring.

5. Open another jump ring and attach one end link of each remaining chain and half the clasp. Close the jump ring. Repeat on the other end with the remaining clasp half.

E

6. Slide the toggle loop with dangles over the bar half of the clasp. Center it on the three chains.

SupplyList

both projects
- chainnose and roundnose pliers
- diagonal wire cutters

necklace
- 6 ft. (1.8m) chain, 5mm links
- **3** 8mm faceted beads
- **3** 2-in. (5cm) head pins
- **3** 4mm jump rings
- loop half of toggle clasp, large enough to accommodate three segments of chain
- toggle clasp

earrings
- 3½ in. (9cm) chain, left over from necklace
- **2** 8mm faceted beads
- **2** 2-in. head pins
- pair of earring wires

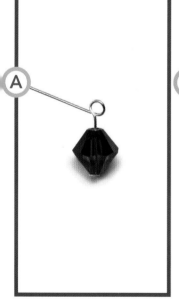

A

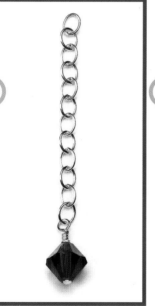

B

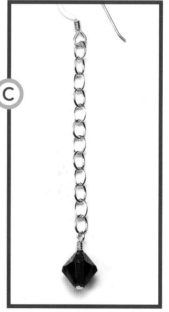

C

earrings • 1. String a bead on a head pin. Make the first half of a wrapped loop above the bead.

Contact Margot in care of BeadStyle.

2. Cut a 1⅝-in. length of chain. Attach the bead unit to an end link of chain. Complete the wraps.

3. Open the loop on an earring wire and attach the end link of chain. Close the loop. Make a second earring to match the first. ❖

Casual coil dangles

Geometric shapes star in these wire earrings

by Wendy Witchner

Shape the base of these distinctive earrings with a few twists and turns, coiling geometric shapes from a single piece of wire. For a professional touch, hammer custom head pins and sculpt your own earring wires. Once you try your hand at these earrings, you'll see how rewarding wire work can be.

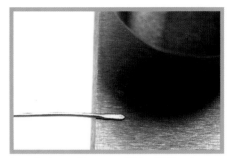

head pins • Cut two 1½-in. (3.8cm) pieces of round wire. Hold one wire so that ⅛ in. (3mm) rests on the bench block or anvil. Hammer the tip of the wire several times until it forms a paddle shape. File the edges. Repeat on the second wire.

earring wires • Cut two 1½-in. pieces of round wire. At one end of one wire, make a plain loop. Bend the wire ⅛ in. above the loop. Using your fingers and chainnose pliers, curve the wire into a question-mark shape, as shown above. Trim the excess wire and file the end. Use chainnose pliers to make a slight upward bend at the end of the wire. File the end. Repeat on the second wire.

Ⓐ

earrings • **1.** Cut two 9-in. (23cm) pieces of twisted wire. File the ends.

2. With roundnose pliers, make a small loop on one wire. Position the chainnose pliers across the loop. Using your fingers, continue coiling the wire to form a spiral. Leave ⅛ in. between each coil; make one full curve around the inner loop.

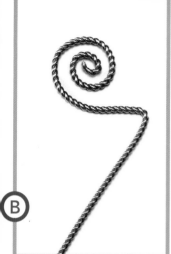

B

3. With chainnose pliers, bend the wire downward, as shown.

C

4. Bend the wire at ¾-in. (2cm) intervals, forming a triangle.

D

5. Make a triangular coil by continuing to bend the wire, leaving approximately ⅛ in. between each coil. Trim the excess wire and file the end.

E

6. Hammer the wire earring form several times. Turn the form over and repeat on the other side.

Make a second wire form to match the first. When finished, turn the form over, so the two pieces are mirror images of each other.

F

7. String a spacer, an accent bead, and a spacer on a head pin. Make a plain loop (Basic Techniques, p. 12). If using a custom head pin, make the loop perpendicular to the paddle. Repeat on the second head pin.

G

8. Open the loop on a dangle and attach it to the bottom of a wire form. Close the loop. Repeat on the second form.

H

9. Open the loop on an earring wire and attach it to the wire form, as shown. Close the loop. Repeat to finish the second earring. ❖

Contact Wendy in care of BeadStyle.

Supply List

- 1½ ft. (46cm) 20-gauge twisted wire, (Thunderbird Supply Co., 800-545-7968, thunderbirdsupply.com)
- 2 6-9mm accent beads
- 4 2-3mm round spacers
- 6 in. (15cm) 20-gauge round wire, half hard or 2 1½-in. (3.8cm) head pins and a pair of earring wires
- ball-peen hammer
- bench block or anvil
- metal file or emery board
- chainnose and roundnose pliers
- diagonal wire cutters

Beau jangles

Wire dainty beads to metal bracelets or earrings for up-to-the-minute style • **by Brenda Schweder**

Although these baubles are timeless, bangle bracelets are particularly *au courant* when embellished with tiny beads. Try a single silver sliver, or wire two or three together and stack an armful. You'll love the earrings, too – handmade teardrops boast sparkling glass, crystal, and gemstone bits. Both fun and refined, these wire trinkets add a great twist to your style.

SupplyList

both projects
- spool of 30-gauge wire
- chainnose pliers
- diagonal wire cutters

bracelets
- assorted 2-4mm gemstones and crystals
- 3 or more 60-63mm bangle bracelets (Fire Mountain Gems, 800-355-2137, firemountaingems.com)
- 22-gauge wire, half-hard
- diagonal wire cutters

earrings
- assorted 2-4mm gemstones and crystals
- 16 in. (41cm) or more 22-gauge wire, half-hard
- 2 or more 1½-in. (3.8cm) head pins or eye pins, 24-gauge
- pair of earring wires (optional)
- roundnose pliers
- spool, ¾-in. (2cm) or larger diameter (use a dowel or 35mm-film canister for different sizes of earrings)
- metal file or emery board

bracelet • 1. Cut a 30-in. (76cm) piece of 30-gauge wire. Wrap one end around a bangle tightly three or four times. Trim the excess wire. String a bead and wrap the wire around the bangle every ⅛ in. (3mm) or so. String beads at ½-in. (1.3cm) intervals or as desired. To finish, make several wraps around the bangle. Trim the excess wire.

2. Cut a 1½-in. (3.8cm) piece of 22-gauge wire. Stack the beaded bangle with one or two plain bangles. Between two beads, tightly wrap the wire around all the bangles two or three times. Trim the excess wire from both ends and gently squeeze each end down with chainnose pliers.

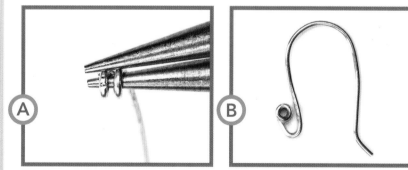

earring wires • 1. Cut a 2-in. (5cm) piece of 22-gauge wire. Using the tip of your roundnose pliers, make two small coils at one end of the wire.

2. Approximately ⅛ in. from the coil, bend the wire upward to make a small loop. Using your fingers and chainnose pliers, curve the wire into a horseshoe shape. Trim the excess wire and file the end. Use chainnose pliers to make a slight upward bend at the wire's end. Repeat steps 1 and 2 to make a second earring wire.

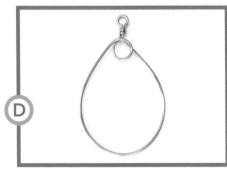

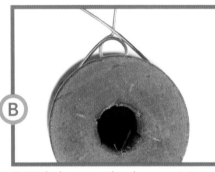

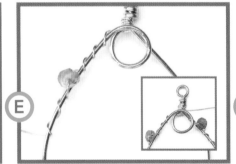

A

B

C

earrings • **1.** Cut a 6-in. (15cm) piece of 22-gauge wire. With the largest part of your roundnose pliers, make the first half of a wrapped loop (Basic Techniques, p. 12) 1½ in. from one end.

2. With the stem (the shorter wire) pointing upward, place the bottom of the loop against a spool and wrap the remaining wire around the spool. Remove the spool.

3. Wrap the wire around the stem, as if completing a wrapped loop. Trim the excess wire.

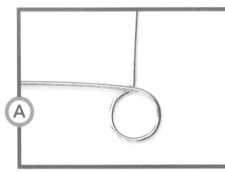

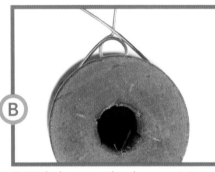

D

E

F

4. Make a plain loop (Basic Techniques) with the wire stem.

Brenda offers the bracelets and earrings in kits. Contact her at Miss Cellany Jewelry Kits, b@brendaschweder.com, or visit brendaschweder.com.

5. Cut a 12-in. (30cm) piece of 30-gauge wire. Wrap one end around the wrapped loop's stem several times. Then wrap the wire around the form, stringing beads at ¼-in. (6mm) intervals.

Wrap the end around the stem of the wrapped loop several times. Trim the excess wire and press the end close to the wraps with chainnose pliers.

6. Open an earring wire's loop and attach the wire form. Close the loop.

7. String a bead on a head pin or eye pin. Make a plain loop above the bead. Open the loop and attach it to the inner loop on the wire form. Make a second earring the mirror image of the first. ❖

Shapely hoops

Combine curved tube beads with beading wire for flowing earrings.

by Don E. Wolford

Post earring findings are commonly used to dangle a beaded head pin. Here's a different technique using beading wire. This method not only gives you the freedom to vary the earring's diameter and combine beads of various shapes and sizes, but also keeps the ear nut conveniently attached.

Contact Don in care of BeadStyle.

1. For an earring with a 1½ in. (38mm) diameter, cut a 5½ in. (.14m) piece of beading wire. String a crimp bead, a 3mm round bead, and an earring post's loop. Go back through the beads just strung and make a folded crimp (Basic Techniques, p. 12).

2. String an 8mm round bead over the crimp. String a 3mm round, a curved tube, and a 3mm round.

3. String a 6mm round, a 3mm round, a tube, a 3mm round, and a 10mm round.

    Start with a 3mm round, and reverse the pattern in step 3, then step 2. End with an 8mm round bead.

4. String a 3mm round bead, a crimp bead, a 2mm round bead, and an ear nut. Go back through the beads just strung, tighten the wire, fold the crimp bead, and trim the excess wire. Make a second earring to match the first. ❖

Supply List

- **2** 10mm round beads
- **4** 8mm round large-hole beads
- **4** 6mm round beads
- **20** 3mm round beads
- **2** 2mm round beads
- **8** 12mm curved tube beads (Rio Grande, 800-545-6566, riogrande.com)
- flexible beading wire, .014 or .015
- **2** 1mm crimp beads
- pair of 4mm ball post earrings with loops
- pair of ear nuts
- chainnose pliers
- diagonal wire cutters

Bend a beautiful
bangle to
showcase a
favorite bead
by Wendy Witchner

Hinged handwork

Necessity is the mother of
invention. For an art bead
to be the focus of a bangle
bracelet, the weightier
beaded section must be
kept on top of the wrist. By
hinging the two wire
pieces and shaping the
bottom portion, the bead
section stays where it will
garner the attention. The
hook-and-eye closure is
placed inconspicuously
opposite the hinge.

*Art beads in the bracelets above: Angi
Graham of The Bluefrog Studio, (254)
965-6005, bluefrog@ourtown.com. Art
bead in the step-by-step shots: Heart
Bead, (707) 441-0626, heartbead.com.*

1. Cut a 5-in. (.13m) piece of 18-gauge plain wire. Fold the 24-gauge twisted wire
in half and rest the fold on the plain wire. Hold the tail and half of the twisted wire
tightly in one hand. With the other hand, wrap the twisted wire tightly around the
core. After a few twists, hold the coiled wire with nylon-jaw pliers. When you've
finished wrapping one end, repeat with the remaining wire, forming a 1½-in. (3.8cm)
coil. (You'll use approximately 8 in./20cm of twisted wire to make 1 in./2.5cm of
coil.) Slide the coil off the wire. Cut the coil into six ¼-in. (6.4mm) segments.

2. Make a 3mm-diameter plain loop (Basic Techniques, p. 12) at one end of the
5-in. piece of 18-gauge wire. Slide a coil, spacer, coil, 8mm bead, coil, bead cap,
art glass bead, bead cap, coil, 8mm bead, coil, spacer, and coil on the wire.

C

D

E

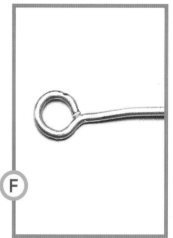

F

3. Bend the wire at a right angle at the end of the last coil. Bend the wire end around your roundnose pliers into a hook. Bring it around to meet the last coil; trim the wire at that point.

4. With roundnose pliers, bend ⅛ in. (3mm) of the wire back and pinch it flush against the hook.

5. Place the hook on a bench block or anvil. Hammer one side to strengthen it. Smooth the hook tip with a file or emery board, if necessary.

6. Place the bead section on your wrist. To calculate the length of the bottom section of the bracelet, measure the underside of your wrist from loop to hook of the bead section, leaving a little ease. Add 1½ in. and cut a piece of 16-gauge plain wire to that length. Make a plain loop at one end.

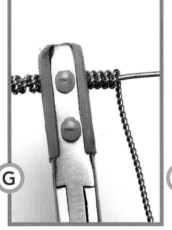

G

H

I

7. Wrap 20-gauge twisted wire on the 16-gauge core wire as in step 1. Work from the middle toward the loop, sliding the coil as necessary. Coil the second half of the twisted wire until the coil covers the core wire. Trim the excess twisted wire.

Contact Wendy in care of BeadStyle.

8. Open the loop on the bead section and link it to the bottom section's loop. Close the loop.

9. Place the bracelet around your wrist and shape it to fit comfortably. Determine where the closure loop should be to accommodate the hook. Cut the wires, allowing ¾ in. (1.9cm) for a loop. Trim the coiled wire so ¾ in. of the core wire is exposed. Make a plain loop parallel with the loop at the opposite end. Hammer the loop as in step 5. ❖

Supply List

- 15-22mm art glass bead
- **2** 8mm accent beads
- **2** 4mm spacer beads
- **2** bead caps to fit art bead
- 1 ft. (.30m) 24-gauge twisted wire (all wire from Thunderbird Supply Co., 800-545-7968, thunderbirdsupply.com)
- 5 ft. (1.52m) 20-gauge twisted wire
- 5 in. (.12m) 18-gauge plain wire
- 6 in. (.15m) 16-gauge plain wire
- roundnose, chainnose, and nylon-jaw pliers
- hammer
- bench block or anvil
- metal file or emery board
- diagonal wire cutters

Woven elegance

Jewel-tone satin cord takes on a new look when accompanied by handsome chain and a coordinating Venetian-glass bead. Once you create your own version, you'll appreciate the versatility of this beautiful necklace. For work, wear it with a fine-gauge turtleneck and your favorite suit. For post-work fun, wear it with a wrap sweater, a circle skirt, and a pair of the season's new curvy heels. Regardless of the outfit, your choice is sure to be enchanting.

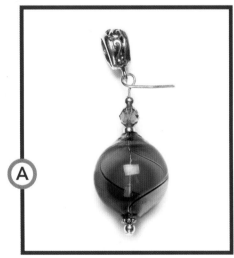

A

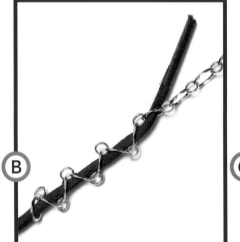

B

C

1. String a head pin with an accent bead or spacer. Then string a Venetian glass bead, accent bead, and spacers, as desired. Make the first half of a wrapped loop (Basic Techniques, p. 12) above the top bead.

2. Attach the loop to the bail and complete the wraps.

3. Put tape, Fray Check, or nail polish on each end of the satin cord. Thread the cord through each large link in the chain.

Determine the finished length of your necklace. (These are 17 in./43cm.) Cut the chain to that length, leaving a large link on each end. Trim each end of the satin cord approximately 1 in. (2.5cm) longer than the chain.

4. Center the pendant on the woven chain.

by Anne Nikolai Kloss

Thread satin cord through chain
for a sophisticated necklace

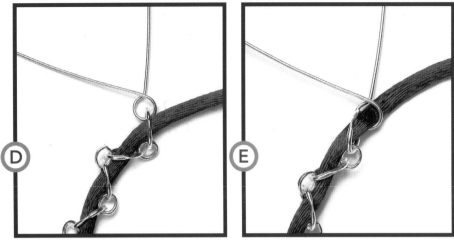

D

E

5. Cut a 4-in. (10cm) length of 22-gauge wire. Make the first half of a wrapped loop approximately 1½ in. (3.8cm) from one end. The loop must be large enough to accommodate the satin cord. Attach the loop to the last link on one end of the chain, then thread the cord through the loop.

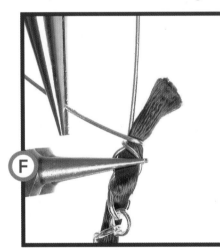

F

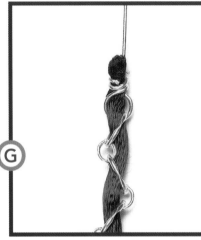

G

6. With the shorter wire, tightly wrap the cord to the loop's stem. Trim the cord ¼ in. (6mm) past the wraps and apply Fray Check or nail polish to the end.

SupplyList

- 2 ft. (61cm) satin cord
- 2 ft. chain with large and small links (large links should accommodate the diameter of the cord)
- Venetian glass bead
- **1-3** crystal accent beads, 4-8mm
- bail with a hole large enough to accommodate the wrapped cord (Rio Grande, 800-545-6566, riogrande.com)
- **2** 3-4mm flat spacers
- **4** or more 3mm round spacers
- **2** beading cones, bottom openings large enough to fit over the wrapped cord
- 3-in. (7.6cm) head pin
- 8 in. (20cm) 22-gauge wire
- S-clasp and **2** soldered jump rings
- chainnose and roundnose pliers
- diagonal wire cutters
- scissors
- Dritz Fray Check or clear nail polish

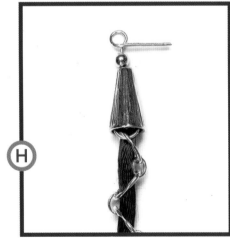

H

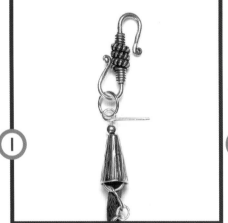

I

J

7. String a cone and a round spacer onto the wire stem. Make the first half of a wrapped loop above the spacer.

8. Attach the loop to a soldered jump ring. Complete the wraps.

9. Loop one end of the S-clasp through the jump ring and close the clasp.

10. Check the fit. If necessary, cut the chain to shorten the necklace. Finish the other end as in steps 5 through 8. ❖

Contact Anne at annekloss@mac.com.

by Georgia Hadley
Branching out

Curve then connect headpins into fanciful earrings

Whether a dressy pair with crystals or an organic pair with tiny nuggets, these pretty earrings will take only twenty minutes to make, tops – simply assemble a trio of beads on curved head pins. So go out on a limb and grow your earring collection with several easy pairs!

Contact Georgia at georgia@adorneya.com or visit adorneya.com.

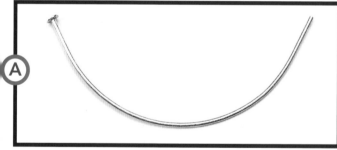

1. Bend a head pin around the cylindrical object. Make a total of three curved head pins.

SupplyList

- 6 3-5mm beads
- 6 1½-in. (3.8cm) 24-gauge head pins
- pair of earring wires
- chainnose and roundnose pliers
- diagonal wire cutters
- dowel, marker, or other cylindrical object, approx. 15mm in diameter

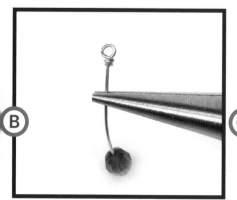

2. String a bead on a curved head pin. Make a small (2-3mm) wrapped loop (Basic Techniques, p. 12) ½-¾ in. (1.3-2cm) from the bead.

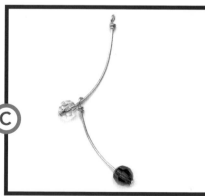

3. String a bead on a second curved head pin, then go through the wrapped loop on the previous head pin. Make sure the head pins curve in opposite directions. Make a small wrapped loop ½-¾ in. from the bead.

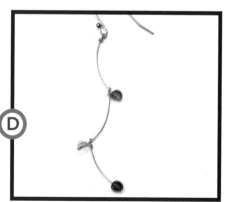

4. Repeat step 3 with a third curved head pin. Open an earring wire and attach the dangle. Close the wire. Make a second earring to match the first. ❖

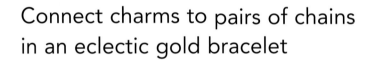

All a-tangle

Connect charms to pairs of chains in an eclectic gold bracelet

by Brenda Schweder

With jumbled pieces of chain, this bracelet might remind you of the tangled mess at the bottom of your jewelry box. Here, however, the effect is deliberate: jump rings connect the chains at various points along the bracelet, creating an asymmetrical drape. Highlighting two trends, this style marries the layered chain look with the continued popularity of the charm bracelet.

A

B

C

1. Determine the finished length of your bracelet. Cut a segment of cable chain (the top chain) to that length. Cut two additional decorative chain segments: a middle chain 1¼ in. (3.2cm) longer than the top and a bottom chain 3 in. (7.6cm) longer than the top.

2. String each bead or charm that cannot be attached by a jump ring on a head pin. Make a wrapped loop (Basic Techniques, p. 12) above each bead.

3. Open an oval jump ring (Basic Techniques) and string the end links of the top, middle, and bottom chains, then a charm. Close the jump ring. On the other end, use an oval jump ring to attach the clasp to all three chains.

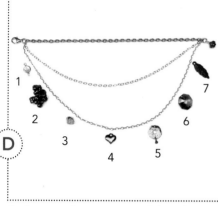

D

E

SupplyList

- 6½-8 in. (16.5-20cm) cable chain, 4-7mm links
- 18-20 in. (46-51cm) decorative chain, two styles, 8-9 in. (20-23cm) of one and 10-11 in. (25-28cm) of the other
- 8 assorted beads and charms, 6-30mm
- 8 1½-in. (3.8cm) gold-filled 24-gauge head pins or 5mm round jump rings to attach charms (plus extras if attaching two-hole beads or charms)
- 2 gold-filled 4mm oval jump rings
- lobster claw clasp
- chainnose and roundnose pliers
- diagonal wire cutters

4. Arrange the seven remaining charms along the chains, balancing colors, finishes, shapes, and sizes. Align the fourth charm with the center of the bottom chain.

5. Open a round jump ring and string the center charm through the center links in the top and middle chains. Close the jump ring.

F

G

6. Attach the second and sixth charms with jump rings to the top and bottom chains, at a point halfway between the center charm and the bracelet's ends. Leave uneven amounts of chain hanging on each side.

7. Attach the remaining charms to the chains, linking pairs of chains together as desired. For two-hole charms, attach each loop to different pairs of chains. Check the fit, and trim an equal number of links from each end, if necessary. ❖

Brenda offers kits for the bracelets. Contact her at Miss Cellany Jewelry Kits, b@brendaschweder.com, or visit brendaschweder.com.

EDITOR'S TIP

Make sure the top chain remains untangled as you attach charms. The bracelet will be too short if the top chain becomes tangled.

Layers of links

Transform lengths of chain into a fashion staple • **by Linda Augsburg**

Coco Chanel popularized the layered, unstructured look of the multistrand chain necklace. She was known to deconstruct and reconstruct jewelry, mixing components until she achieved just the right look for her personal accessories. Coco's love of chain even extended to her clothing line – sewing chain into the hemlines of Chanel jackets ensured their perfect drape.

Inspired by those Chanels, this chain necklace combines sterling and Bali silver beads in a classic layered combination. The chain-only bracelet can stand alone as a quick fashion addition, while the dangling earrings subtly mimic the necklace.

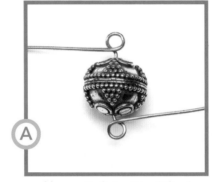

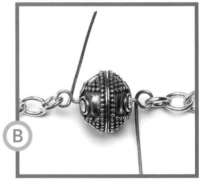

necklace • 1. Cut a 4-in. (10cm) piece of wire. String a bead on the wire and make the first half of a wrapped loop (Basic Techniques, p. 12) at each end. Make a total of five units.

Determine the finished length of the shorter and longer strands. (The shorter strands in this necklace are 18 in./46cm; the longer strands, 24 in./61cm.) Cut one piece of fine chain to each length and two pieces of medium chain to the longer length. Set aside.

2. Cut four 1⅝-in. (4.1cm) segments of medium chain. To make the center portion, attach a chain segment's end link to each loop of a 13mm bead unit.

C

D

3. Link an 11mm bead unit to the end links of the center portion. Then, link a 1⅝-in. segment to each end. Link a 13mm bead unit to each end.

Measure the center portion and subtract that number from the shorter strand length. Cut a segment of medium chain to that length. Cut this segment in half and attach each to the end bead units. Complete the wraps.

4. Attach the end link of the three longer chains to one split ring and the end link of the two shorter chains to another split ring. Attach each ring to a loop on half the box clasp.

Repeat on the other end with the other clasp half. Check the fit, and trim equal amounts of chain from each end if necessary.

bracelet • **1.** Determine the finished length of the bracelet. Subtract the length of the clasp. Cut two pieces of medium chain and one piece of fine chain to that length.

2. Attach each chain's end link to a split ring. Attach each split ring to a clasp half.

A

B

earrings • **1.** String a bead on a decorative head pin. Make the first half of a wrapped loop above the bead.

2. Cut a 1¼-in. (3.2cm) segment of fine chain. Slide an end link on the loop and complete the wraps.

3. Open an earring wire's loop, string the chain's end link, and close the loop.

Repeat steps 1 through 3 to make a matching earring. ❖

Supply List

necklace
- 5½ ft. (1.7m) medium chain, 4-5mm
- 4 ft. (1.2m) fine chain, 2-3mm
- 5 Bali silver beads, **3** 13mm and **2** 11mm
- 2 ft. (61cm) 22-gauge wire, half hard
- **4** 5mm split rings
- two-strand box clasp
- chainnose and roundnose pliers
- diagonal wire cutters
- split-ring pliers (optional)

bracelet
- 12-16 in. (30-41cm) medium chain, 4-5mm
- 6-8 in. (15-20cm) fine chain, 2-3mm
- **2** 5mm split rings
- box clasp
- diagonal wire cutters
- split-ring pliers (optional)

earrings
- 3 in. (7.6cm) fine chain, 2-3mm
- **2** 11mm Bali beads
- **2** 1½-in. (3.8cm) decorative head pins
- pair of earring wires
- chainnose and roundnose pliers
- diagonal wire cutters

E

4. String an accent bead on a head pin. Make a plain loop above the bead.

5. Open the loop on the dangle and attach it to the coil's bottom loop. Close the dangle's loop.

F

6. Open an earring wire and attach the coil's top loop. Close the earring wire. Make a second earring the mirror image of the first (to make the coil, twist the wire in the opposite direction from the first coil). ❖

Shapely spirals

Coil wire to create earrings • by Lea Nowicki

Make sophisticated spiral earrings by coiling wire around a pen and hanging an accent bead at one end. Experiment with the type of wire (such as square or twisted), the number and spacing of the wraps, or the size of the pen to create a variety of coils. Let your creativity spiral out of control to put your own twist on these stylish earrings.

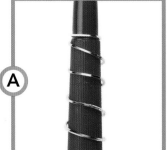

A

1. Determine the length of each finished coil, multiply by four, and cut two pieces of wire to that length. (For example, cut a 6-in./15cm piece of wire to make a coil 1½ in./3.8cm in length.) Wrap the wire tightly around the pen barrel. Remove the wire coil.

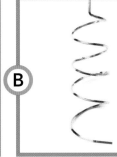

B

2. If desired, adjust the coil's shape with your fingers. Bend ⅜ in. (1cm) of the wire upward at a right angle.

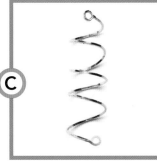

C

3. Make a plain loop (Basic Techniques, p. 12) at the top end of the coil. If necessary, trim excess wire at the bottom of the coil, allowing ⅜ in. for a plain loop. Make a plain loop.

SupplyList

- 2 4-8mm accent beads
- 12-18 in. (30-46cm) 20- or 22-gauge wire, half hard
- 2 1-in. (2.5cm) head pins
- pair of earring wires
- chainnose and roundnose pliers
- diagonal wire cutters
- pen with a graduated barrel

Contact Lea in care of BeadStyle.

Links and lace

Wrapped loops connect gemstone buttons and filigree in a delicate necklace and earrings

by Jill Italiano

With its fine metal work, detailed filigree jewelry will assume its place among the ladylike bijoux in your collection. For this double-strand necklace, you'll make many small, beaded links, so you may need several work sessions. Be patient and make the loops round and the wraps tight; the results will be well worth your time. Another design option: Use a little more wire and string three buttons (rather than two) on each link. The necklace will retain its delicate look but will come together more quickly.

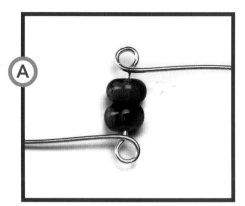

necklace • 1. Cut a 2-in. (5cm) piece of wire. String two gemstone buttons and make the first half of a wrapped loop (Basic Techniques, p. 12) ⅛ in. (3mm) from each bead. Make a total of 59 bead units. Depending on the desired necklace length, you may need a few more or less. (The shorter strand in this necklace is 15 in./38cm, with 27 bead units; the longer, 18 in./46cm, with 32 units.)

2. Attach a 4mm soldered jump ring to each loop on one bead unit. Complete the wraps.

3. To make the shorter strand, link one loop on a bead unit to the previous jump ring, and the other loop to a 4mm soldered jump ring. Complete the wraps. Repeat until the strand is within 1½ in. (3.8cm) of the desired length, ending with a soldered jump ring. Set aside.

D

4. Open a 4mm jump ring (Basic Techniques) and string a 4mm soldered jump ring and a filigree's loop. Close the jump ring.

E

5. To make the longer strand: Attach a loop from two bead units to the soldered jump ring. Link a 4mm soldered jump ring to each of the remaining loops. Complete the wraps.

F

6. Continue attaching links and jump rings as in step 3, until the strand is within 1½ in. of the desired length. End with a 4mm soldered jump ring on each side.

7. Open a 4mm jump ring. String the end ring of both strands and a 6mm soldered jump ring. Close the jump ring. Repeat on the other end. Check the fit. If necessary, add or remove an equal number of links from each end. (If you remove a 4mm soldered jump ring from one of the ends, link a 4mm jump ring through the remaining wrapped loop.)

8. Attach an S-hook clasp to one of the 6mm jump rings. Close half the clasp with chainnose pliers.

SupplyList

both projects
• chainnose and roundnose pliers
• diagonal wire cutters

necklace
• filigree, approx. 20mm
  (The Bead Shop, 650-328-7925,
  beadshop.com)
• 16-in. (41cm) strand 4mm gemstone
  buttons, pearl or obsidian
• 10-13 ft. (3-4m) 24-gauge wire,
  half hard
• **65-80** 4mm soldered jump rings
• **3-7** 4mm jump rings
• S-hook clasp and **2** 6mm soldered
  jump rings

earrings
• **6** 4mm gemstone buttons, pearl
  or obsidian
• **2** filigrees, approx. 20mm
• **6** 1½-in. (3.8cm) eye pins or
  decorative head pins
• pair of earring wires

earrings • 1. String a gemstone button on an eye pin or decorative head pin and make the first half of a wrapped loop above the bead. Make a total of six dangles.

2. Attach a dangle to one loop on a filigree. Complete the wraps. Attach a dangle on each side of the first dangle and complete the wraps.

Contact Jill at jill@bellaoro.com or visit jilldesigns.com.

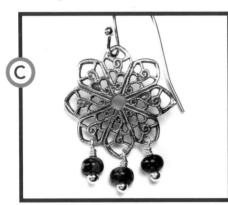

3. Open an earring wire and attach the top loop on the filigree. Close the earring wire. Make a second earring to match the first. ❖

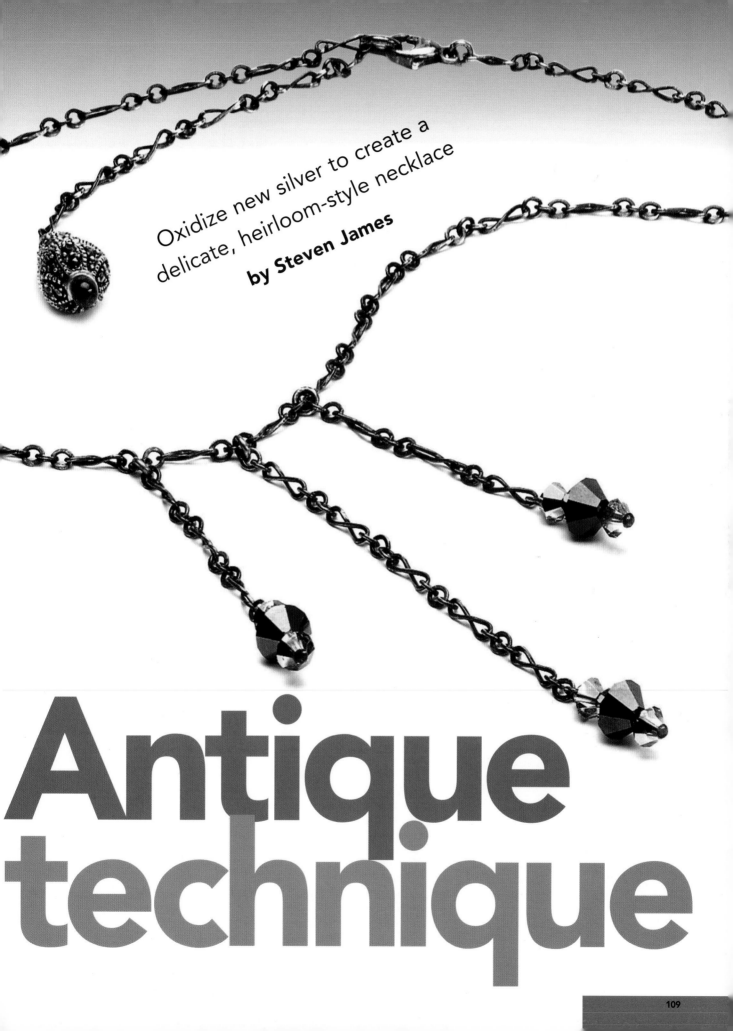

Oxidize new silver to create a delicate, heirloom-style necklace

by **Steven James**

Antique technique

Transform a shiny, contemporary necklace into one with the mysterious air of a bygone era. The secret lies in a 15-second process that alters new silver, producing a dramatic metamorphosis.

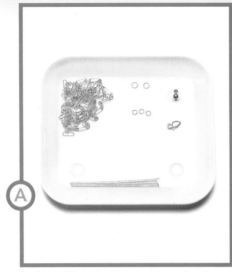

1. Determine the finished length of your necklace. (This one is choker length – 15 in./38cm, with a 3-in./7.6cm dangle.) Cut a piece of chain to the necklace length, cutting through a long link of chain. Cut two 2½-in. (6cm) and two 1¼-in. (3cm) lengths of chain for the dangles. Gather all the sterling silver components.

2. Read the Black Max directions thoroughly. Following the directions, dip the chain, jump rings, spacers, clasp, and head pins in the solution for 15 seconds. Remove the items and wash with a mild detergent. Rinse the pieces and let them dry completely. Use a furniture-polish wipe to apply a light coat of wax; this protects the black finish.

Supply List

- 2 ft. (61cm) sterling silver chain, 3mm triple long and short
- **3** 6mm bicone crystals
- **6** 4mm bicone crystals
- **6 x 14mm** teardrop-shaped bead, marcasite
- 4mm spacer bead, sterling silver
- 3mm spacer bead, sterling silver
- **4** 1½-in. (38mm) head pins, sterling silver
- **4** 3mm jump rings, sterling silver
- lobster claw clasp and 5mm jump ring, sterling silver
- chainnose and roundnose pliers
- diagonal wire cutters
- Midas Black Max (Rio Grande, 800-545-6566, riogrande.com)
- pre-moistened furniture polish wipe, such as Pledge Wipes

3. String each of three head pins with a 4mm crystal, a 6mm crystal, and a 4mm crystal. Make a plain loop (Basic Techniques, p. 12) above the top crystal on each. Open the loops and attach one dangle to each 1¼-in. chain segment and one to a 2½-in. chain segment. Close the loops.

4. Open a 3mm jump ring (Basic Techniques) and attach the 2½-in. dangle to the center of the necklace. Close the jump ring. Attach each of the two 1¼-in. dangles with a 3mm jump ring to the middle link of the small-link section of chain on each side of the center dangle.

E

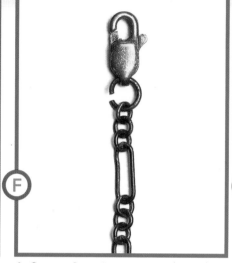

F

G

5. String a head pin with a 3mm spacer, a marcasite drop, and a 4mm spacer. Make the first half of a wrapped loop (Basic Techniques) above the top bead. Slide the dangle onto the end link of the remaining 2½-in. piece of chain. Complete the wraps and trim the excess wire. Dab a bit of Black Max on the cut end of the wire. Be careful not to get Black Max on the marcasite.

6. Open a 3mm jump ring and attach the clasp to one end of the necklace chain. Close the jump ring.

7. Open the 5mm jump ring and attach it to the other end of the necklace and the end link of the marcasite drop. Close the jump ring. ❖

Contact Steven at Beadissimo, (415) 282-2323, or seamus@beadissimo.com.

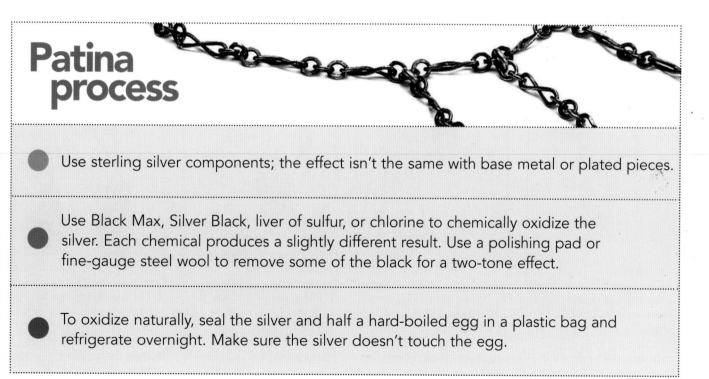

Patina process

- Use sterling silver components; the effect isn't the same with base metal or plated pieces.

- Use Black Max, Silver Black, liver of sulfur, or chlorine to chemically oxidize the silver. Each chemical produces a slightly different result. Use a polishing pad or fine-gauge steel wool to remove some of the black for a two-tone effect.

- To oxidize naturally, seal the silver and half a hard-boiled egg in a plastic bag and refrigerate overnight. Make sure the silver doesn't touch the egg.

by Brenda Schweder

It's a

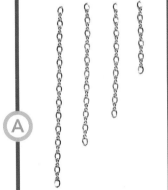

(A)

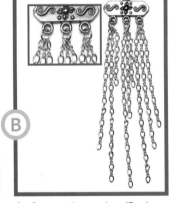

(B)

(C)

(D)

1. Cut pairs of chain segments in assorted lengths for each connector bar's hanging loop. (These range from 1¼ to 2¾ in./ 32 to 70mm.) Reserve one segment from each pair for the second earring.

2. Open a jump ring (Basic Techniques, p. 12) and link it to a connector loop. String groupings of three or more segments on each jump ring; close the jump rings.

3. String beads on head pins as desired and make the first half of a wrapped loop above the bead (Basic Techniques).

4. For top-drilled beads, cut a 2½-in. (64mm) piece of wire. String a bead and make a set of wraps above it (Basic Techniques).

Make the first half of a wrapped loop ⅛ in. (3mm) above the wraps.

breeze

Whip up cascade earrings in a flurry of seasonal colors

The price of some earrings will blow you away. Challenge yourself to create a pair sans the inflated price tag. Designing is a breeze when you attach all the chain segments first, then arrange the placement of gemstones and crystals on this curtain of chain. Try summery watercolors in peridot, aquamarine, and tanzanite or muted fall hues of garnet, carnelian, and berry quartz.

E

5. Attach dangles as desired, staggering their placement along each chain segment. Complete the wrapped loops.

F

6. Open the loop on an earring wire and attach the top loop of the connector bar. Close the earring wire loop.

Make a second earring the mirror image of the first, using the remaining chain segments. ✤

Supply List

quantities will vary
- 3-8 ft. (.91-2.44m) cable or figure-eight chain, approx. 2mm
- assorted gemstones and crystals, 3-12mm
- 2 connector bars (gold bars from The Beadin' Path, 877-922-3237, beadinpath.com; silver bars from Rio Grande, 800-545-6566, riogrande.com)
- 1½-in. (38mm) plain or decorative head pins
- 24-gauge wire, half-hard
- 3-4mm jump rings
- pair of earring wires
- chainnose and roundnose pliers
- diagonal wire cutters

Brenda offers the gold earrings as a kit. Contact her at Miss Cellany Jewelry Kits, b@brendaschweder.com, or visit brendaschweder.com.

Make a
statement with
gold chain in a
long necklace
and earrings

by **Jane Konkel**

Chain

Anywhere you go, you can spot lengthy chain necklaces – some even dipping below the hip. Why not sport your own long chain look? Here, crystal flowers with scalloped edges nestle in the necklace's tidy web of draped chain. The earrings' detailed filigree mirrors this scalloped pattern. Drizzled sparingly with sapphire blue crystals, these pieces are a minimalist's must-have.

EDITOR'S TIP

No need for a clasp: Your necklace is long enough to slip over your head. If you make a shorter necklace, omit the 24-in. (61cm) chain. Instead, cut two pieces of chain to the desired length and attach a clasp.

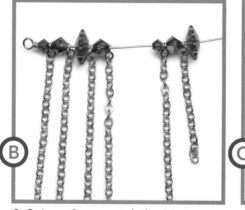

necklace • 1. Cut eight pieces of chain, one to each of the following lengths: 24, 12, 6, 5, 4, 3, 2, and 1 in. (61, 30, 15, 13, 10, 7.6, 5, and 2.5cm, respectively).

2. Cut a 4-in. piece of wire and make a wrapped loop (Basic Techniques, p. 12) at one end.

3. String a 3mm crystal, the 6-in. chain's end link, 4mm crystal, 5-in. chain, saucer, 4-in. chain, 4mm crystal, and the 3-in. chain. String a 3mm crystal, 2-in. chain, 4mm crystal, 1-in. chain, and a saucer.

4. String the 1-in. chain's remaining end link. Beginning with a 4mm crystal, reverse the pattern in step 3, stringing each remaining chain's end link and ending with a 3mm crystal. Make a wrapped loop next to the end crystal.

couture

D

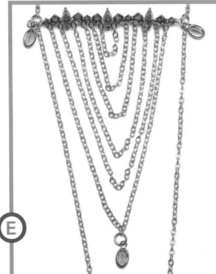

E

5. Open a jump ring (Basic Techniques). String one end link of the 24-in. chain, a crystal channel, one end link of the 12-in. chain, and a wrapped loop. Close the jump ring. Repeat, joining the opposite ends of the chains to the remaining wrapped loop.

6. Open a jump ring and attach a channel to the center link of the 6-in. chain. Close the jump ring.

Supply List

necklace
- **5 ft.** (1.5m) 1.5-2.5mm chain
- **4 in.** (10cm) 24-gauge gold-filled wire, half hard
- **4** 3mm bicone crystals
- **6** 4mm bicone crystals
- **3** 8mm crystal flower saucers
- **3** 6 x 4mm oval crystal channels (Rio Grande, 800-545-6566)
- **3** 3mm or 4mm jump rings
- chainnose and roundnose pliers
- diagonal wire cutters

earrings
- **2** filigrees with loops, approx. 20mm (Jan's Jewels and More, 405-840-2341, jansjewels.com)
- **9 in.** (23cm) 1.5-2.5mm chain
- **2** 8mm crystal flower saucers
- **8** 6 x 4mm oval crystal channels
- **2** 1½-in. (3.8cm) decorative head pins
- **14** 3mm or 4mm jump rings
- pair of earring wires
- chainnose and roundnose pliers
- diagonal wire cutters

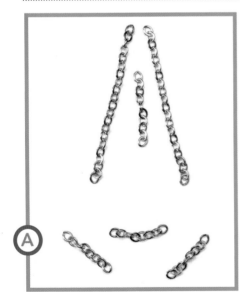

A

B

C

earrings • 1. Cut pieces of chain to the following lengths: two 1½, one ¾, and three ½ in. (3.8, 2, and 1.3cm, respectively).

2. String a saucer on a head pin and make a plain loop (Basic Techniques) above the crystal.

3. Open the loop and attach the ¾-in. chain's end link. Close the loop.

4. Open a jump ring and string a ½-in. chain's end link, a crystal channel, and a filigree's loop. Close the jump ring. Repeat on the opposite side.

5. Open two jump rings. On each, string an end link of the remaining ½-in. chain, a channel, and the end link of chain (from step 4). Attach each jump ring to the filigree as shown. Close each jump ring.

D

6. Open a jump ring and string a 1½-in. chain's end link and a filigree's loop. Close the jump ring. Repeat on the opposite side.

E

7. Open a jump ring and string a 1½-in. chain's end link, ¾-in. chain with dangle, and the remaining 1½-in. chain's end link. Close the jump ring.

F

8. Open an earring wire and string the top jump ring. Close the earring wire. Make a second earring to match the first. ❖

G

Seductive SWIRLS

Craft curvy earrings by shaping wire

by Wendy Witchner

A few simple twists with your pliers will transform wire into sexy earrings. Cut glass or gemstone dangles swing saucily below the earrings' graceful curves, flashing a spark of color.

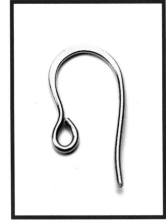

earring wires • Cut a 1½-in. (3.8cm) piece of wire. At one end, make a plain loop (Basic Techniques, p. 12). Bend the wire ⅛ in. (3mm) above the loop. Using your fingers and chainnose pliers, curve the wire into a question-mark shape. Hammer each side. Trim the excess wire and file the end. Repeat to make a second earring wire.

(A)

earrings • 1. Cut a 3½-in. (9cm) piece of wire. File the ends. With roundnose pliers, make a small loop at each end of the wire. The loops should curve toward each other.

Supply List

- 11 in. (28cm) 20-gauge round wire, half-hard
- 2 2-2.5mm round beads
- 2 single-loop 6 x 4mm or 10 x 8mm Wrap-Tites and 2 faceted glass or gemstones to set in them or 2 preset Swarovski channels (Rio Grande, 800-545-6566)
- pair of earring wires or 3 in. (7.6cm) 20-gauge round wire, half-hard
- chainnose and roundnose pliers
- diagonal wire cutters
- ball-peen hammer
- bench block or anvil
- metal file or emery board

(B)

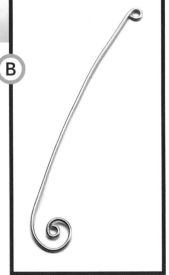

2. Position the chainnose pliers across one loop to hold it in place. Using your fingers, coil one end of the wire to form a spiral, making almost one full rotation around the small loop.

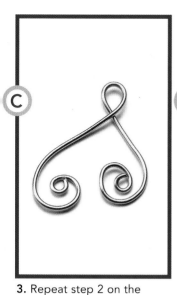

C

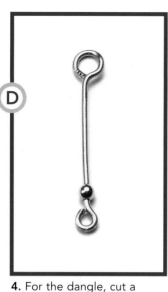

D

E

F

3. Repeat step 2 on the other end of the wire. To make the top loop, twist a loop in the wire just off-center. The spirals should be at different heights, both facing inward. If desired, hammer the shape several times on each side.

4. For the dangle, cut a 1¼-in. (3.2cm) piece of wire. File both ends. With your roundnose pliers, make a small plain loop (Basic Techniques) at one end. String a round bead on the wire and make a large plain loop at the other end.

5. If using a Wrap-Tite and stone, set the stone in the Wrap-Tite. Open the small loop on the dangle. String the set stone or channel on the small loop and close the loop. Open the dangle's large loop and attach it to the shape's top loop. Close the loop.

6. Open the loop on an earring wire and attach it to the shape's top loop. Close the loop. Make a second earring the mirror image of the first. ❖

Contact Wendy in care of BeadStyle.

Who's got the button?

Showcase vintage buttons in a wire-wrapped earring

by Wendy Witchner

Turn spectacular buttons into fashionable earrings by framing a button with a spiral of wire. Hammer and antique the spiral to mirror the button's vintage style. Unable to find vintage buttons? Not to worry. Check local fabric stores for wonderful reproductions.

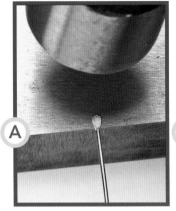

A

1. To make a head pin, cut a 1-in. (2.5cm) piece of wire. Place ⅛ in. (3mm) of the wire on a bench block or anvil. Hammer the tip of the wire several times until it forms a paddle shape. Smooth the edges with a file.

B

2. String a 2mm spacer, 4mm crystal, spacer, 6mm crystal, and a spacer on the head pin. Make a plain loop (Basic Techniques, p. 12) above the bead, perpendicular to the paddle.

C

3. Cut a 7-in. (18cm) piece of wire. Make a loop in the wire and thread it through the button's shank. Wrap the wire around the shank. Forming the wire with pliers and your fingers, bring it out to the edge (this will be the top) and spiral it around the perimeter of the button, encircling it 1½ times.

D

4. Make a small V-shaped bend in the wire at the bottom of the second coil.

E

5. Complete the second coil. Trim the wire approximately ½ in. (1.3cm) beyond the top. With roundnose pliers, turn a small loop in the opposite direction of the spiral. The loop and the V-shaped bend should be aligned.

Contact Wendy in care of BeadStyle.

F

6. Remove the button by opening the loop. Place the outer coils of the spiral on the bench block or anvil and hammer them to add texture and to strengthen the shape.

If desired, antique the wire with a blackening agent, following the manufacturer's instructions.

G

7. Reattach the button and reshape the spiral.

Open the loop on the crystal dangle, attach it at the V-shaped bend, and close the loop.

H

8. Open the loop on the earring wire, attach the top loop of the earring, and close the loop.

Make a second earring the mirror image of the first. ❖

SupplyList

- 2 ¾-⅞-in. (2-2.2cm) buttons with shanks
- 2 6mm bicone crystals
- 2 4mm bicone crystals
- 6 2mm round spacers
- 18 in. (46cm) 22-gauge wire, half-hard

- pair of earring wires
- ball-peen hammer
- metal file or emery board
- bench block or anvil
- chainnose and roundnose pliers
- diagonal wire cutters
- blackening agent (Black Max) or liver of sulfur (optional)

Connect jump rings and
seed beads into a necklace
and earring combo

by Karin Buckingham

Lots of links

Heavy-gauge rings
have a modern appearance,
and linked together, they
make casual, contemporary
jewelry. Open the rings only as
far as necessary so they'll
maintain their shape and close
easily. Because sterling silver is
soft, protect the rings with a
cloth to prevent damage from
your tools. You'll quickly find
your linking rhythm and have
fun making this set.

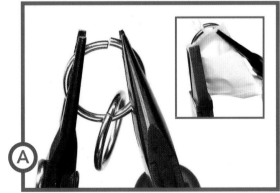

A

necklace • **1.** Open a 13mm jump ring (Basic
Techniques, p. 12), slide on a second jump ring,
and close the first. To prevent marring, protect
the rings with a cloth (see inset). Repeat until the
necklace is within 1 in. (2.5cm) of the desired
length. (This one is 16½ in./42cm.)

B

2. To make dangles,
open five 10mm jump
rings and string three
seed beads on each.

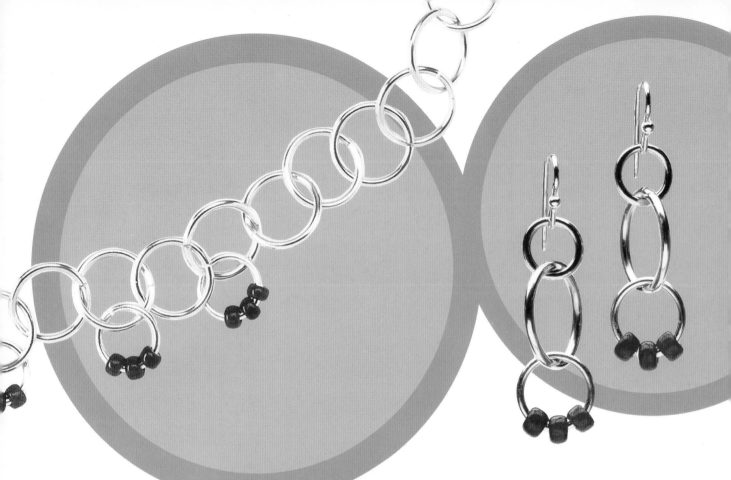

3. Fold the chain in half to find the center link. Attach one dangle to the center jump ring. On each side, attach a dangle to every other ring.

4. On one end of the necklace, open a 13mm jump ring and attach the jump ring to a lobster claw clasp. On the other end, open a 13mm jump ring and attach an 8mm soldered jump ring. Close the jump rings.

SupplyList

both projects
- **2** pairs of pliers, chainnose and either roundnose or bentnose

necklace
- **31** or more 13mm 14-gauge jump rings, (Rio Grande, 800-545-6566, riogrande.com)
- **5** 10mm 14-gauge jump rings
- **15** size 6º seed beads
- lobster claw clasp with jump ring
- **8mm** soldered jump ring

earrings
- **2** 13mm 14-gauge jump rings
- **2** 10mm 14-gauge jump rings
- **6** size 6º seed beads
- **2** 8mm soldered jump rings
- pair of earring wires

Contact Karin in care of BeadStyle.

earrings • 1. Make a dangle unit as in step 2 for the necklace, using a 10mm jump ring and three seed beads.

2. Open a 13mm jump ring. Attach a dangle unit and a 8mm soldered jump ring. Close the jump ring.

3. Open an earring wire and attach the soldered loop. Close the earring wire. Make a second earring to match the first. ❖

Shortcuts

Readers' tips to make your beading life easier

1 paper-cup pouring

Roll beads from your work surface into a small paper cup, flatten the sides, and pour the beads into their storage container. This low-cost solution is efficient and prevents beads from spilling.
– Nancy McKee,
San Ysidro, CA

2 project scrapbook

Keep track of your projects in a beading scrapbook: On a sheet of paper, write down a materials list. In the top corner, staple a few leftover beads in a small, resealable bag. Then, tape a photo of the finished piece to the bottom of the page. Add project notes (such as the cost or helpful tips). Finally, insert the page into a sheet protector and file it in a three-ring binder. The scrapbook is especially useful if you sell or give away many of your finished pieces.
– Erika Barrientes,
Brownsville, TX

3 oval jump rings

For extra security when a project calls for unsoldered jump rings, substitute oval jump rings: A clasp, pendant, or charm will hang safely away from the jump ring's opening, making it less likely to detach accidentally.
– Sandra Porter,
via e-mail

4 storage to go

For secure, visible storage, stack beads and findings in plastic cups with clear covers. Save the containers from restaurant takeout, or purchase them in bulk from a discount store. For added convenience, organize the cups on a revolving tray.
– Susan Van Voorhees,
Columbia, MD

5 tarnished reputation

Buy vintage chains at thrift stores or rummage sales. You'll find some great deals as well as a variety of colors and finishes not otherwise available. Then, mix and match old and new chains to create a fantastic new piece.
– T. Sebastian, via e-mail

Gemstones

String gemstone chips with seed beads for a quick and easy jewelry set

by **Maria Camera**

Chip & trendy

A liberal dose of gemstone chips achieves lighthearted appeal in a graceful necklace. Chips are easy to match with seed beads and crystals to produce a mellow monochromatic palette. The necklace pattern translates easily to earrings or a quick bracelet.

necklace • 1. To make the dangle's bottom unit, string a focal bead, a flat spacer, and a seed bead on a decorative head pin. Make the first half of a wrapped loop (Basic Techniques, p. 12) above the top bead.

To make the dangle's top unit, cut a 3½-in. (9cm) piece of 22-gauge wire. Make a wrapped loop at one end. String two gemstone chips, a spacer, a crystal, a spacer, two chips, and a seed bead. Make a wrapped loop perpendicular to the bottom loop.

2. Attach the dangle's bottom unit to the bottom loop of the dangle's top unit. Complete the wraps.

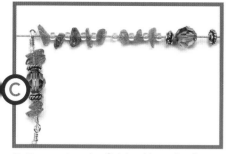

3. Determine the finished length of your necklace. (These are 17 in./43cm.) Add 6 in. (15cm) and cut a piece of beading wire to that length. Center the dangle on the wire.

On each side of the dangle, string an alternating pattern of eight chips and eight seed beads, a spacer, a crystal, and a spacer. Repeat on each end until the necklace is within 1 in. (2.5cm) of the desired length. Because chips can vary in size, check to see that both ends are equal in length.

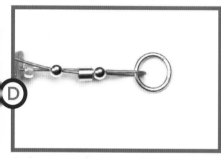

4. On one end, string a 2mm round, a crimp bead, a round, and a soldered jump ring. Go back through the last beads strung. Repeat on the other end, substituting a lobster claw clasp for the soldered jump ring. Tighten the wires, check the fit, and add or remove an equal number of beads from each end if necessary. Crimp the crimp beads (Basic Techniques) and trim the excess wire.

Supply List

necklace
- 8-12mm focal bead
- 16-in. (41cm) strand 3-5mm gemstone chips
- **9-13** 6mm round crystals
- 1g size 11º seed beads
- **4** 2mm round spacers
- **19-27** 4mm flat spacers
- 3½ in. (9cm) 22-gauge wire, half hard
- 2-in. (5cm) 22-gauge decorative head pin
- flexible beading wire, .014 or .015
- **2** crimp beads
- lobster claw clasp and soldered jump ring
- chainnose and roundnose pliers
- diagonal wire cutters
- crimping pliers (optional)

bracelet
- 3-5mm gemstone chips, left over from the necklace
- size 11º seed beads, left over from the necklace
- **3-5** 6mm round crystals
- **4** 2mm round spacers
- **6-10** 4mm flat spacers
- flexible beading wire, .014 or .015
- **2** crimp beads
- lobster claw clasp and soldered jump ring
- chainnose or crimping pliers
- diagonal wire cutters

earrings
- **2** 8-12mm focal beads
- **8** 3-5mm gemstone chips, left over from the necklace
- **2** 6mm round crystals
- **4** size 11º seed beads, left over from the necklace
- 7 in. (18cm) 22-gauge wire, half hard
- **2** 2-in. 22-gauge decorative head pins
- **6** 4mm flat spacers
- pair of earring wires
- chainnose and roundnose pliers
- diagonal wire cutters

Contact Maria in care of BeadStyle.

bracelet • Determine the finished length of your bracelet, add 5 in. (13cm), and cut a piece of beading wire to that length. Repeat the pattern in step 3 of the necklace until the bracelet is within 1 in. of the desired length. Follow step 4 to finish the bracelet.

earrings • 1. Make a dangle following steps 1 and 2 of the necklace.

2. Open the loop on an earring wire and attach the dangle. Close the loop. Make a second earring to match the first. ❖

Gemstones in four shapes and colors unite in a bold multistrand necklace

by Diana Grossman

You'll cover all the bases in one striking necklace by mixing gemstone shapes, sizes, and colors. Select the most unusual shape first, then more common shapes; different gemstones are not always available in the same cuts. Keep the sizes within a couple of millimeters of the first shape chosen to make the necklace well-balanced. Finally, choose a pendant in proportion with the gemstones' sizes. Follow these basic guidelines to score a colorful and captivating accessory.

GRAND

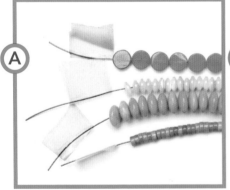

A

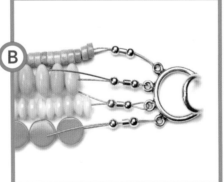

B

C

1. Determine the finished length of your necklace. (The jewel-toned necklace is 16 in./41cm; the pastel is 18 in./46cm.) Add 6 in. (15cm) and cut four pieces of beading wire to that length.

2. Tape one end of each wire. String each beaded strand on a beading wire until the necklace is within 1 in. (2.5cm) of the desired length.

3. On one end of each wire, string a 3mm round spacer, a crimp bead, a spacer, and the respective loop on half the clasp. Go back through the beads just strung and tighten the wire. Remove the tape and repeat on the other end. Check the fit. If necessary, add 3mm round spacers to lengthen or remove gemstones to shorten. Crimp the crimp beads (Basic Techniques, p. 12) and trim the excess wire.

4. Open a jump ring (Basic Techniques) and string it through the pendant's loop. Close the jump ring.

STRANDS

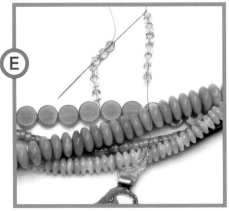

5. Thread a beading needle with a 7-in. (18cm) piece of Fireline. String approx. 5 in. (13cm) of 3mm or 4mm beads. Center the pendant on the strand.

6. Encircle the necklace with the beaded Fireline. Go back through all the beads, exiting from the last bead strung. To make the pendant detachable, string enough beads on the Fireline to maneuver over the strands and clasp.

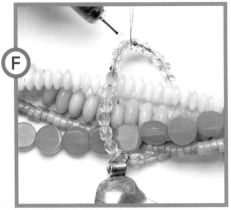

7. Tie the ends in a surgeon's knot (Basic Techniques). Trim the Fireline to ⅛ in. (3mm) and apply glue to the knot. Gently maneuver the knot inside an adjacent bead. ❖

Contact Diana at
jewels@deenmiele.com.

Supply List

- pendant, top drilled
- **4** 16-in. (41cm) strands 4-10mm gemstones, four shapes and colors
- **16–18** 3mm or 4mm faceted round Czech crystals
- **16** or more 3mm round spacers
- 7mm jump ring
- flexible beading wire, .014 or .015
- Fireline fishing line, 6 lb. test
- **8** crimp beads
- four-strand clasp
- beading needle, #10
- GS Hypo Cement
- chainnose and roundnose pliers
- diagonal wire cutters
- scissors

Delicately balanced

by Rupa Balachandar

Coral and silver combine in this lightweight necklace

Angel skin coral, dyed a deep shade of peach, is a refreshing alternative to conventional red coral. Pair it with dainty silver dangles to make an easy, ethereal necklace.

A

1. Determine the finished length of your necklace. (This one is 17 in./43cm). Add 6 in. (15cm) and cut a piece of beading wire to that length.

String a rounded bead dangle, four 4mm rounds, a daisy dangle, and four rounds. String a flat spacer. Repeat the pattern three more times, separating each section with a flat spacer. Center the beads on the wire.

B

2. String a flat spacer, 6mm accent bead, and a flat spacer on each end.

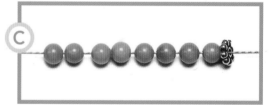

C

3. String eight 4mm rounds and a spacer on each end. Repeat once. String 4mm rounds on each end until you are within 1 in. (2.5cm) of the desired length.

D

4. String a 2mm round spacer, a crimp bead, a round, and half the clasp. Go back through the beads just strung. Repeat on the other end with the remaining clasp half. Tighten the wire and check the fit. Add or remove an equal number of beads on each end, if necessary. Crimp the crimp beads (Basic Techniques, p. 12) and trim the excess wire. ❖

Contact Rupa at rupa_balachandar@hotmail.com or visit her website, rupab.com.

SupplyList

- 16-in. (41cm) strand 4mm round angel skin coral
- **11** 3mm flat spacers
- **4** 4mm silver daisy dangles
- **2** 5 x 6mm silver accent beads
- **4** 2mm round spacer beads
- flexible beading wire, .014 or .015
- **2** crimp beads
- toggle clasp
- chainnose or crimping pliers
- diagonal wire cutters

Mobility

Sculpt freeform wire earrings and highlight with gemstones

by Steven James

Alexander Calder, the American kinetic sculptor, revered strong colors, geometric shapes, and the natural world. Miniature wearable mobiles were inspired by this artist. Each is made with one continuous piece of wire shaped by hand. Faceted teardrops or rondelles are the best accents for the wire, as they really catch the light.

Supply List

- **2** 10 x 20mm briolettes, faceted gemstones, or crystals
- **2** 10 x 12mm briolettes, faceted gemstones, or crystals
- **1** ft. (.30m) 22-gauge sterling silver wire
- pair of earring wires
- roundnose and chainnose pliers
- diagonal wire cutters

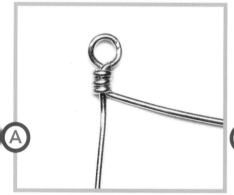

1. Cut a 6-in. (15cm) piece of wire. Make a wrapped loop (Basic Techniques, p. 12) in the middle of the wire.

2. Using your fingers, curve the wire into a wishbone shape. With chainnose pliers, make a right angle on one side about 1½ in. (3.8cm) from the loop.

3. Slide the larger stone onto the wire. Make a right angle bend in the wire on the other side of the stone.

4. Cross the wires into an X, then bend the short wire so it is perpendicular to the longer wire.

5. Wrap the short wire around the long wire twice as in a wrapped loop. Trim the excess wire. Reshape the earring, if necessary.

Contact Steven at Beadissimo, (415) 282-2323, or seamus@beadissimo.com.

6. Make a right angle with the other wire, about ¾ in. (2cm) from the top loop. Repeat steps 3 through 5 using the smaller stone. The direction of this loop should be perpendicular to the longer wire's loop.

Open the loop on an earring wire and attach the earring. Close the loop. Make a second earring the mirror image of the first. ❖

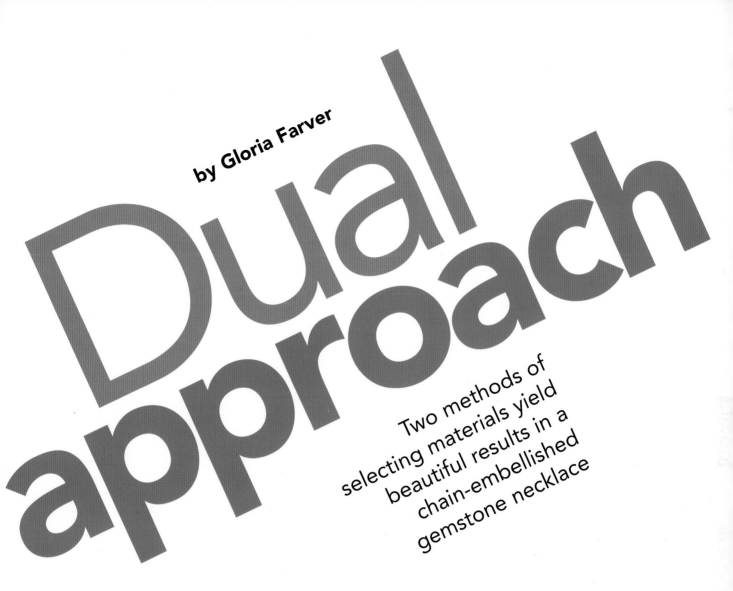

Dual approach

by Gloria Farver

Two methods of selecting materials yield beautiful results in a chain-embellished gemstone necklace

Coordinating versus complementary beads poses a fundamental question when selecting materials to accompany a pendant. Create a monochromatic look by using one stone, such as moss agate, in various shapes — a pear-shaped pendant, faceted rondelles, and oval accent beads. Or, highlight the subtle hues in a multicolor pendant with accents in complementary rather than coordinating colors. Consider also the varieties of chain and spacers: The green necklace features a large-link chain and slightly thicker spacers, while the pink necklace has a small-link chain and therefore daintier spacers. Once you select your materials, the stringing will take very little time, with impressive results.

1. String a 2mm round spacer, crystal, spacer, crystal, and a spacer on a head pin. Make the first half of a wrapped loop (Basic Techniques, p. 12) above the spacer. On each of two head pins, string a round spacer, a crystal, and a spacer. Make the first half of a wrapped loop on each.

B

2. Cut a ½-in. (1.3cm) piece of chain, making sure to have an even number of links. Attach each dangle, with the longer one in the middle, to the end link. Complete the wraps.

C

3. Cut two ¾-in. (2cm) pieces of chain. Open a 3mm or 4mm jump ring (Basic Techniques) and string an end link of each piece of chain and the dangle. Close the jump ring.

D

4. Determine the finished length of your necklace. (The green necklace is 18 in./46cm; the pink, 17 in./43cm.) Add 6 in./15cm and cut a piece of beading wire to that length. Center a seed bead, a crystal, the pendant, a crystal, and a seed bead on the wire. String one side of the chain dangle on each end. If the chain has large links, string the end links over the seed beads. If desired, trim the chains to adjust how the dangle hangs.

EDITOR'S TIP

Requiring less than 3 in. (7.6cm) of chain, this project makes handy use of remnants. Just make sure the links are large enough to accommodate three dangles.

E

5. On each end, alternate four rondelles with four seed beads, then string a crystal, flat spacer, oval, spacer, crystal, and a seed bead. Repeat twice (three times for a longer necklace).

F

6. On each end, string rondelles interspersed with seed beads until the necklace is within 1 in. (2.5cm) of the desired length. Then, string a round spacer, a crimp bead, a spacer, and half the clasp on each end. Go back through the last beads strung and tighten the wires. Check the fit, and add or remove beads from each end if necessary. Crimp the crimp beads (Basic Techniques) and trim the excess wire. ❧

SupplyList

both projects
- flexible beading wire, .014 or .015
- chainnose and roundnose pliers
- diagonal wire cutters
- crimping pliers (optional)

green necklace
- pendant, approx. 31 x 44mm, top drilled, moss agate
- **6-8** 13 x 18mm oval beads, moss agate
- 16-in. (41cm) strand 5 x 8mm rondelles, moss agate
- **18-22** 4mm bicone crystals, shadow crystal
- 1g size 11º seed beads
- **12-16** 7mm flat spacers
- **11** 2mm round spacer beads
- 3 in. (7.6cm) silver chain, 5mm links
- 3-4mm jump ring
- **3** 1½-in. (3.8cm) head pins
- **2** crimp beads
- box clasp

pink necklace
- pendant, approx. 26 x 47mm, top drilled, ocean jasper
- **6-8** 10 x 15mm faceted oval beads, moonkite
- 16-in. strand 6 x 10mm rondelles, pink jade
- **18-22** 4mm bicone crystals, Ceylon topaz
- 1g size 11º seed beads
- **12-16** 6mm flat spacers
- **11** 2mm round spacer beads
- 3 in. silver chain, 2mm links
- 3-4mm jump ring
- **3** 1½-in. head pins
- **2** crimp beads
- toggle clasp

Contact Gloria at rfarver@wi.rr.com.

S·t·r·e·t·c·h
above the rest

by Paulette Biedenbender

Slide on a tailored, elastic bracelet

Convey a quiet elegance by wearing this sleek, stretchable bracelet. Moss agate is the chosen stone for this version, enhanced with silver beads.

1. Double your wrist measurement, add 5 in. (13cm), and cut two pieces of elastic to that length. Thread a beading needle, and string one strand through a rectangular bead's top holes, alternating with a round bead until you've strung the desired length. End with a round bead. String the second strand through the bottom holes, repeating the pattern.

2. Check the fit. Add or remove beads, if necessary. Tape three of the ends. Thread the needle on the last strand.

3. To connect the beads, insert the needle, in the same direction, through the first rectangular bead strung.

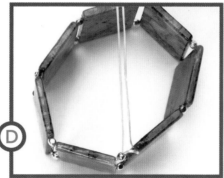

4. Continue through the remaining beads along this edge of the bracelet, exiting from the last bead strung. The bracelet will take on a circular shape.

5. Remove the tape from one of the strands along the bracelet's other edge. Repeat steps 3 and 4.

6. Tie a surgeon's knot (Basic Techniques, p. 12) between a round and a rectangular bead with two adjacent strands. Dot the knot with glue and allow to dry. Trim the excess elastic. Hide the knot by pulling gently on the adjacent beads to maneuver it inside the rectangular beads.

Repeat on the other edge with the remaining strands. ✤

Supply List

- 16-in. (41cm) strand two-holed rectangular beads, 20 x 31mm
- **14** or more 2mm round silver beads
- 3 ft. (.91m) ribbon elastic
- twisted-wire beading needle, #10
- G-S Hypo Cement
- scissors

Contact Paulette in care of BeadStyle.

Gemstone

Two gemstone strands intertwine in a sophisticated
necklace and earrings • **by Lea Nowicki**

turnabout

Beautiful alone but even better together, individual strands of pearls and faceted gemstones combine to form a dazzling rope necklace. Two tricks make for a graceful, tapered twist. First, select similarly sized pearls and gemstones to ensure that both have equal prominence in the finished piece. Second, align the strands so one extends farther than the other on each end. Save two top-drilled beads for earrings and add a cluster of accent beads, and your jewelry will look polished, but not overdone.

necklace • **1.** Determine the finished length of your necklace. (The green and gold necklace is 16 in./41cm; the pink and white necklace, 19 in./48cm.) Add 8 in. (20cm) and cut two pieces of beading wire to that length. On one wire, string 13½ in. (34cm) of briolettes or round beads. (For a shorter necklace, string 11 in./28cm of beads.) Make sure each bead faces the opposite direction of the preceding bead.

2. On the second wire, string pearls to the same length as the previous strand.

3. On one end of each wire, string 2½ in. (6.4cm) of accent beads. On the other end of each wire, string 1½ in. (3.8cm) of accent beads. (For a shorter necklace, string 2¼ and 1¼ in./ 5.7 and 3.2cm, respectively.) Reverse one of the strands to stagger the center beads. Tape each end.

4. Cut a 3½-in. (9cm) piece of 22-gauge wire. Make a wrapped loop (Basic Techniques, p. 12) at one end.

Twist the strands together and check the fit, allowing 1½ in. for finishing. Remove the tape, and add or remove beads from each end if necessary.

On one end of each strand, string a crimp bead, a round spacer, and the wrapped loop. Go back through the beads just strung plus a few more. Tighten the wires, crimp the crimp beads (Basic Techniques), and trim the excess beading wire. Repeat on the other end.

5. String a cone and a 5mm bead on one wire. Make the first half of a wrapped loop above the bead. Repeat on the other end.

6. Attach each loop to a clasp half and complete the wraps.

Supply**List**

both projects
- chainnose and roundnose pliers
- diagonal wire cutters

necklace
- 16-in. (41cm) strand top-drilled briolettes or round beads, approx. 6 x 11mm
- 16-in. strand top-drilled pearls, approx. 6 x 9mm
- 16-in. strand 3-4mm silver accent beads
- **2** 5mm round beads
- **2** silver cones, approx. 11 x 13mm
- **4** 2-3mm round spacers

- 7 in. (18cm) 22-gauge wire, half hard
- flexible beading wire, .014 or .015
- **4** crimp beads
- toggle clasp

earrings
- **2** top-drilled beads, left over from necklace
- **10** silver accent beads, left over from necklace
- **10** 1-in. (2.5cm) head pins
- 6 in. (15cm) 26-gauge wire, half hard
- pair of earring wires

earrings • 1. String an accent bead on a head pin. Make a plain loop (Basic Techniques) above the bead. Make a total of five dangles.

2. Cut a 3-in. (7.6cm) piece of wire. String a top-drilled bead and make a wrap above it (Basic Techniques). String the dangles on the wire.

3. Make a wrapped loop above the dangles. Open the loop on an earring wire and attach the dangle. Close the earring wire's loop. Make a second earring to match the first. ❖

Contact Lea in care of BeadStyle.

Rethinking
green

Updated color creates a fresh,
new look in this necklace,
bracelet, and earrings

by Naomi Fujimoto

What's old is new again as fashion reinvents colors from the past. In this jewelry set, 1970s avocado reemerges as a more intense hue of peridot green. The overall design is delicate and deceptively simple, with peridot briolettes sprinkled along brilliant strands of tiny, gold seed beads and accompanied by dainty dangle earrings. These pieces convey an understated elegance that centers around the gorgeous green gemstones. The result is a classy color update that is simply unforgettable.

Select and arrange the briolettes for all three projects before you start stringing.

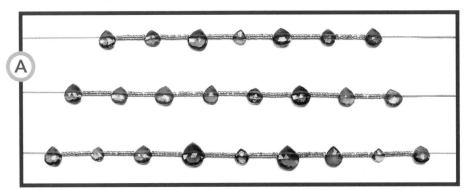

necklace • 1. Determine the finished length of your necklace. (These strands are 14 in., 14¾ in., and 15¾ in./35.6cm, 37.5cm, and 40cm, respectively.) Add 6 in. (15cm) to each measurement and cut a piece of beading wire to each length.

Remove the briolettes from the strand. If you're making earrings, choose two briolettes of equal size and set aside. Divide the remaining briolettes into three groups, one for each strand of the necklace. Arrange the briolettes, alternating sizes and quantities. (This necklace has strands with seven, eight, and nine briolettes.) Set aside two briolettes for the bracelet if desired.

On each wire, string a section of briolettes, interspersed with ten or more seed beads. Center each section on its wire.

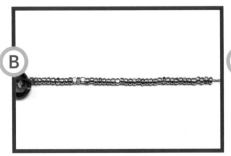

2. On each end of each wire, string seed beads until the strand is within 1 in. (2.5cm) of the desired length. Check the fit, and add or remove an equal amount of beads from each end if necessary.

3. On each end of each wire, string a round spacer, a crimp bead, a round spacer, and the respective loop on a clasp half. Go back through the beads just strung and tighten the wires. Double-check the fit, and add or remove beads from each end if necessary. Crimp the crimp beads (Basic Techniques, p. 12) and trim the excess wire.

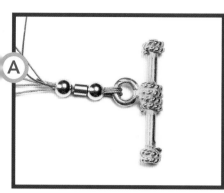

A

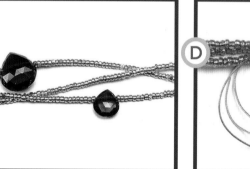

bracelet • 1. Determine the finished length of your bracelet, add 6 in., and cut three pieces of beading wire to that length. String a large-hole spacer, a crimp bead, a spacer, and half the clasp over the three wires. Go back through the beads, tighten the wires, and crimp the crimp bead. Trim the excess wire. If desired, mark the bracelet's halfway point on each wire with a permanent marker.

B

2. On one wire, string seed beads just past the bracelet's halfway point, then string a briolette. String seed beads until the strand is within 1 in. of the desired length. On another wire, string seed beads just short of the bracelet's halfway point, then string a briolette. String seed beads until the strand is within 1 in. of the desired length.

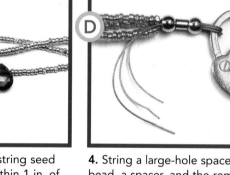

C

3. On the remaining wire, string seed beads until the strand is within 1 in. of the desired length. Loosely braid the three strands.

D

4. String a large-hole spacer, a crimp bead, a spacer, and the remaining clasp half over the three wires. Go back through the beads, tighten the wires, and check the fit. Add or remove beads, if necessary. Crimp the crimp bead and trim the excess wire.

A

earrings • 1. Cut a 2-in. (5cm) piece of 26-gauge wire. String a top-drilled briolette and make a wrapped loop (Basic Techniques) above the bead.

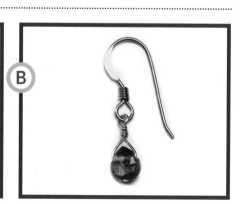

B

2. Open the loop on an earring wire and attach the dangle. Close the loop. Make a second earring to match the first. ❖

Jewelry that's substantive in color and heft can be a refreshing change. Opaque gemstone fans are the perfect starting point, especially in earthy tigereye or green unakite. Stick with natural materials in your wardrobe (such as a suede jacket or feather earrings), and you'll be in your element.

Natural elements

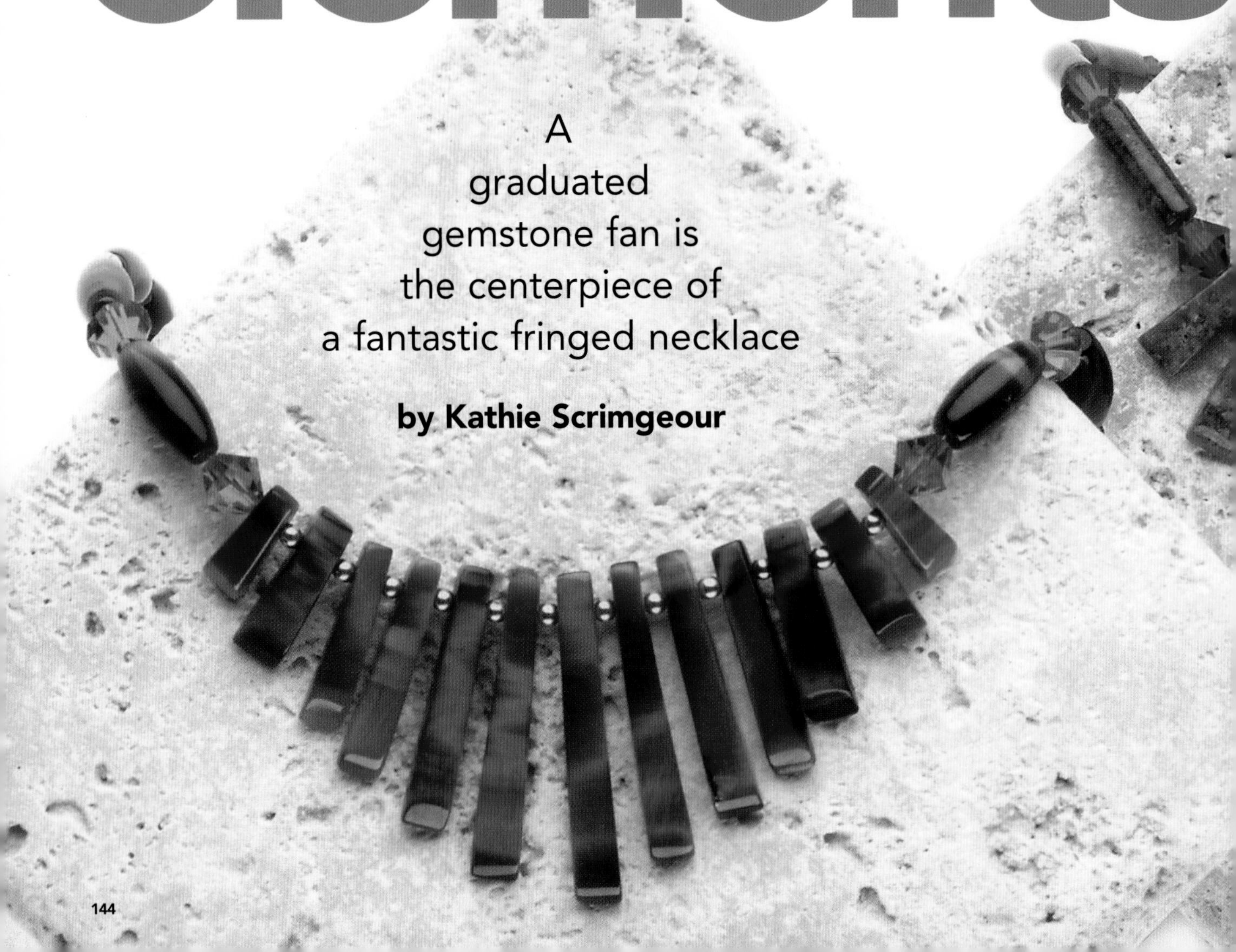

A graduated gemstone fan is the centerpiece of a fantastic fringed necklace

by Kathie Scrimgeour

SupplyList

both projects
- flexible beading wire, .014 or .015
- chainnose or crimping pliers
- diagonal wire cutters

tigereye (brown) necklace
- 13-piece 14-30mm gemstone mini fan, tigereye (Fire Mountain Gems, 800-355-2137, firemountaingems.com)
- 16-in. (41cm) strand 13 x 5mm oval gemstone beads, tigereye
- **4** 6mm bicone crystals
- **6** 4mm round crystals

- **16** or more 2mm round spacer beads
- **4** 3 x 7mm oval beads
- **2** crimp beads
- toggle clasp

unakite (green) necklace
- 13-piece 14-30mm gemstone mini fan, unakite (Fire Mountain Gems)
- 16-in. (41cm) strand 13 x 4mm gemstone tubes, unakite
- **4** 6mm bicone crystals
- **6** 4mm round crystals
- **20** or more 2mm round spacer beads
- **4** 3 x 7mm oval beads
- **2** crimp beads
- toggle clasp

Contact Kathie at (303) 898-1380 or postmaster@crystalcavedesign.com, or visit crystalcavedesign.com.

1. Determine the finished length of your necklace. (The tigereye necklace is 18 in./46cm; the unakite necklace, 16½ in./42cm.) Add 6 in. (15cm) and cut a piece of beading wire to that length. String the fan beads in graduated order interspersed with 2mm round spacer beads. Center the beads on the wire.

2. On each side of the center beads, string a bicone crystal, 13mm bead, bicone, 13mm, oval, 13mm, round crystal, 13mm, and an oval.

3. On each end, string a 13mm bead, round crystal, 13mm, round, and 13mm. String 13mm beads (interspersed with round spacers, if desired) until the necklace is within 1 in. (2.5cm) of the finished length.

4. On one end, string a round spacer, a crimp bead, a round spacer, and half the clasp. Go back through the beads just strung and tighten the wire. Repeat on the other end. Check the fit and add or remove an equal number of beads from each end, if necessary. Crimp the crimp beads (Basic Techniques, p. 12) and trim the excess wire. ❖

Floral
arrangement

Contrasting colors blossom in a striking necklace, bracelet, and earrings

by Kate Purdy

In this multistrand necklace, varying shades of green create a lush setting for a carved flower pendant. The necklace's three-strand gemstone flower pattern shines in a matching bracelet. A pair of earrings also highlights the vibrant colors for an enchanting set.

necklace • **1.** If the pendant has a center hole, string a 6mm spacer, the pendant, and a 3mm bead on a decorative head pin. Bend the head pin as in a wrapped loop (Basic Techniques, p. 12). Complete the wraps around the bead. Trim the excess wire.

2. Cut a 3-in. (7.6cm) piece of 22-gauge wire. String the pendant and make a wrap above it as in a top-drilled bead (Basic Techniques). Make a wrapped loop above the first set of wraps, perpendicular to the pendant.

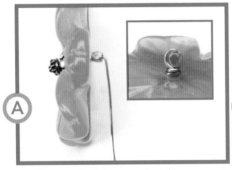

3. Determine the finished length of your necklace. (These are 17½ in./ 44.5cm.) Add 6 in. (15cm) and cut three pieces of beading wire to that length. Center the pendant over all three strands. On each side, alternate four 5mm flat spacers and four 5mm silver beads. String a triangular connector on each end, separating the strands.

4. On the outer strands on each side of the pendant, string a rondelle, 6mm round, rondelle, 6mm, rondelle, 8mm round, rondelle, 6mm, rondelle, 6mm, and a rondelle.

On each end of the middle strand, string a rondelle, 6mm, rondelle, 8mm, 5 x 10mm, 8mm, rondelle, 6mm, and a rondelle. If necessary, string additional rondelles to even out the strands.

E

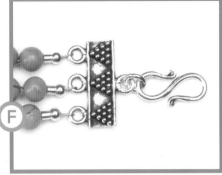

F

A

5. On each side, string a three- or five-strand spacer bar. (If using a five-strand bar, string through the outer and center holes.) String 6mm rounds on each strand until the necklace is within 1 in. (2.5cm) of the desired length.

6. String a crimp bead, a round spacer, and the respective loop of a clasp half on each end of each wire. Go back through the beads just strung plus one more and tighten the wires. Check the fit, and add or remove an equal number of beads from each end, if necessary. Crimp the crimp beads (Basic Techniques) and trim the excess wire.

bracelet • **1.** Determine the finished length of your bracelet, add 5 in. (13cm), and cut three pieces of beading wire to that length.

String the pattern as in step 4 of the necklace, substituting 4 x 6mm rondelles for 6mm rounds. The outer strands should be slightly longer than the middle strand, so string an extra 2 x 3mm rondelle on each end, if necessary. Center the beads. String a triangular connector on each end.

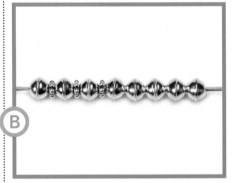

B

2. On each end, alternate three 5mm silver beads with three flat spacers. String 5mm beads until the bracelet is within 1 in. of the desired length.

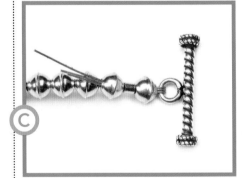

C

3. On each end, string a crimp bead, a 5mm silver bead, and half the clasp. Go back through the beads just strung plus one more. Tighten the wires. Check the fit, and add or remove an equal number of beads from each end, if necessary. Crimp the crimp beads and trim the excess wire.

SupplyList

necklace

- carved flower pendant, approx. 38mm, top drilled (if pendant has a center hole, you'll also need a 6mm flat spacer, a 3mm accent bead, and a 2-in./5cm decorative head pin)
- **8** 8mm faceted beads (cherry quartz beads from SunLight Gems, 310-474-3585, sunlightgems.com; smoky quartz from Planet Bead, 800-889-4365)
- **2** 16-in. (41cm) strands 6mm round faceted beads (amazonite or turquoise)
- **2** 5 x 10mm silver beads
- **32–40** 2 x 3mm rondelles (peridot or olive stone)
- **8** 5mm silver beads
- **2** 12 x 16mm triangular three-to-one connectors (SunLight Gems)
- **2** three- or five-strand spacer bars
- **8** 5mm flat spacers
- **6** 3mm round spacer beads
- **3** in. (7.6cm) 22-gauge sterling wire, half hard
- flexible beading wire, .014 or .015
- **6** crimp beads
- three-strand clasp
- chainnose and roundnose pliers
- diagonal wire cutters
- crimping pliers (optional)

bracelet

- **4** 8mm faceted beads
- **10** 4 x 6mm rondelles (ocean quartz from SunLight Gems; turquoise from Planet Bead)
- **16–20** 2 x 3mm rondelles
- **5** x 10mm silver bead
- **16–20** 5mm silver beads
- **2** 12 x 16mm triangular three-to-one connectors
- **6** 4mm flat spacers
- flexible beading wire, .014 or .015
- **2** crimp beads
- toggle clasp
- chainnose or crimping pliers
- diagonal wire cutters

earrings

- **2** 8mm faceted beads
- **2** 4 x 6mm rondelles
- **2** 2 x 3mm rondelles
- **2** 5mm flat spacers
- **2** 1½-in. (3.8cm) head pins
- pair of earring wires
- chainnose and roundnose pliers
- diagonal wire cutters

(A)

earrings • **1.** String an 8mm round, a 4 x 6mm rondelle, a flat spacer, and a 2 x 3mm rondelle on a head pin. Make a wrapped loop above the top bead.

(B)

2. Open an earring wire and attach the dangle. Close the earring wire. Make a second earring to match the first. ❖

Contact Kate through her website, islandbangles.com.

Faceted nuggets polished to a glossy sheen are bold and enticing. But for some, the cumbersome nature of a chunky necklace outweighs its beauty. No need to resist these tempting morsels any longer. Use the nuggets front and center to keep them as the focus, but alleviate the bulk. Finish your necklace with smaller beads accompanied by deeply hued crystals to preserve the necklace's heavyweight impact.

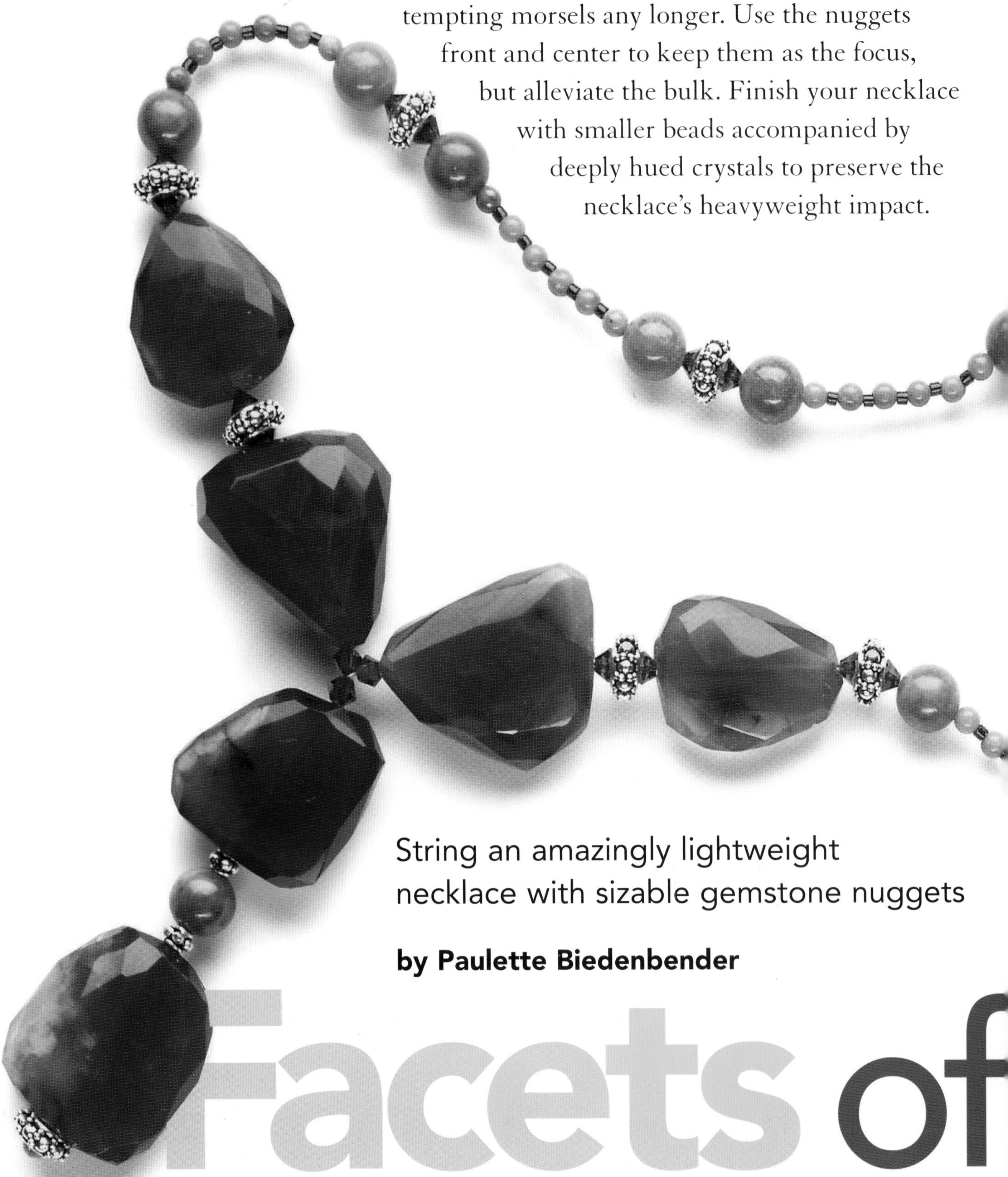

String an amazingly lightweight necklace with sizable gemstone nuggets

by Paulette Biedenbender

Facets of

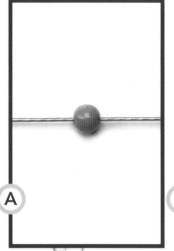

C

4. Separate the wires. On each end, string a crystal, nugget, crystal, 8mm spacer, crystal, and a nugget.

A

1. Determine the finished length of your necklace including the dangle. (This one is 19 in./48cm plus a 3-in./7.6cm dangle.) Add 10 in. (25cm) and cut a piece of beading wire to that length.

2. Center a 3mm round bead on the wire.

B

3. Fold the wire in half around the 3mm bead. On both strands, string an 8mm spacer, nugget, 3 x 2mm spacer, 8mm round, 3 x 2mm spacer, nugget, and a crystal.

Supply List

- 16-in. (41cm) strand faceted agate nuggets (eBeadShop, 770-696-5321, ebeadshop.com)
- 16-in. strand 3mm round beads, rhodochrosite
- **15** 8mm round beads, rhodochrosite
- **23** 4mm bicone crystals
- 1g size 11º Japanese cylinder beads
- **11** 8mm spacers with a 4mm hole
- **2** 3 x 2mm spacers
- **4** 2mm round spacers
- flexible beading wire, .014 or .015
- **2** crimp beads
- hook and eye clasp
- chainnose or crimping pliers
- diagonal wire cutters

D

5. On each end, string a crystal, an 8mm spacer, and a crystal.

Contact Paulette in care of BeadStyle.

E

6. On each end, string an 8mm round, an alternating pattern of six 3mm rounds and five cylinder beads, and an 8mm round.

7. Repeat steps 5 and 6 until the necklace is within 1 in. (2.5cm) of the desired length.

F

8. On each end, string a 2mm round spacer, a crimp bead, a 2mm round spacer, and half the clasp. Go back through the beads just strung and tighten the wire. Check the fit, and add or remove an equal number of beads from each end, if necessary. Crimp the crimp beads (Basic Techniques, p. 12) and trim the excess wire. ✤

distinction

Cinnabar

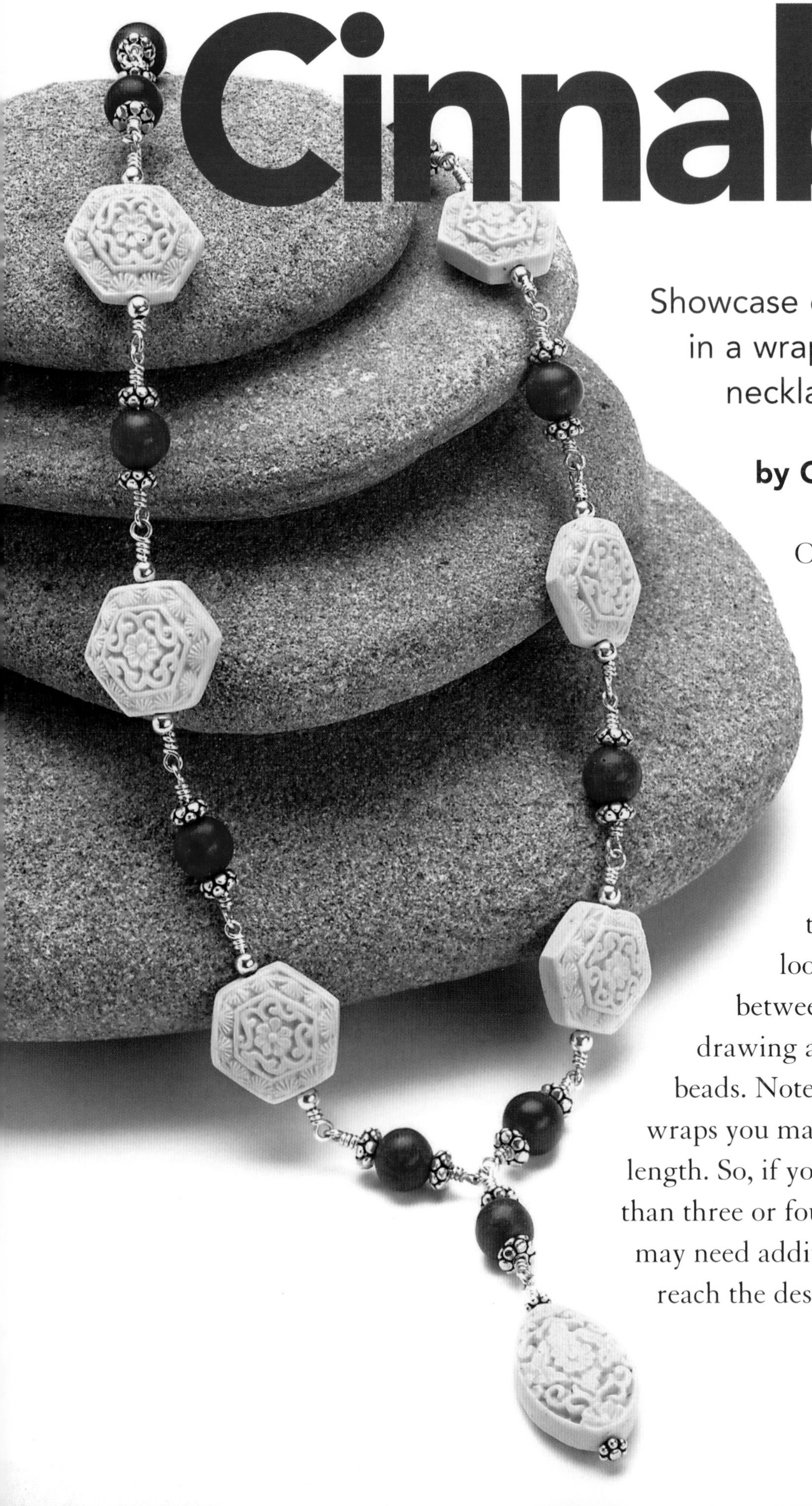

Showcase exotic beads
in a wrapped-loop
necklace

by Gloria Farver

Oval and hexagonal
cinnabar beads are
the starting point
for this project,
but any handful of
noteworthy beads
can become a
necklace through a
wrapped-loop
technique. Wrapped
loops extend the spaces
between components,
drawing attention to individual
beads. Note that the number of
wraps you make affects the necklace
length. So, if you make two (rather
than three or four) wraps per loop, you
may need additional bead units to
reach the desired length.

sensation

1. String a 3mm flat spacer, oval bead, and 3mm spacer on a 2½-in. (6.4cm) head pin. Make the first half of a wrapped loop (Basic Techniques, p. 12) ⅛ in. (3mm) above the beads.

2. Determine the finished length of your necklace. (This one is 16 in./41cm and has 11 round units and 6 hexagonal units, with three wraps per loop.)

Cut a 3-in. (7.6cm) piece of wire. String a 5mm spacer, 8mm round, and 5mm spacer and make the first half of a wrapped loop ⅛ in. from the bead on each end. Make a total of 11 units.

3. Cut a 4-in. (10cm) piece of wire. String a 3mm round spacer, hexagon, and round spacer. Make the first half of a wrapped loop ⅛ in. from the beads on each end. Make a total of six hexagonal bead units.

4. To make the dangle, connect the loop on the oval bead unit with a round bead unit. Complete the wraps.

5. Attach a round unit's loop to the dangle's top loop. Repeat with a second round unit. Complete the wraps.

6. On each end, attach a hexagonal unit, then a round unit. Complete the wraps. Repeat until the necklace is within 2 in. (5cm) of the desired length.

7. On each end, attach the loop of a round unit to the previous unit. On one end, slide a lobster claw clasp onto the remaining open loop. On the other end, slide a soldered jump ring onto the remaining loop. Complete the wraps. ❖

Contact Gloria at rfarver@wi.rr.com

SupplyList

- **15 x 24mm oval bead,** carved white cinnabar (Caravan Beads, 773-248-9555)
- **6 or 8 16mm hexagonal beads,** carved white cinnabar (Caravan Beads)
- **11-15 8mm round gemstones,** apple jasper
- **22-30 5mm flat spacers**
- **12-16 3mm round silver spacers**
- **2 3mm flat spacers**
- **2½-in. (6.4cm) head pin**
- **6½ ft. (2m) 22-gauge wire**
- lobster claw clasp and soldered jump ring
- chainnose and roundnose pliers
- diagonal wire cutters

Take2

A two-strand necklace with a removable pendant serves double duty

by Rupa Balachandar

Creating a necklace that works well with many clothing choices and converts easily from one look to another is a jewelry lover's dream. This piece, which centers around an art bead selected to suit the colors of your wardrobe, accents a favorite twinset or jewel-neck top when worn as a two-strand. For a different look, simply slide the pendant's loop over both strands for an accessory that looks terrific with a V-neck sweater. Blissful versatility!

pendant • 1. Cut a 12-in. (30cm) length of beading wire. String a seed bead or 3mm glass bead and a crimp bead at one end. Pass back through the crimp bead. Tighten the wire and make a folded crimp (Basic Techniques, p. 12). Trim the excess wire.

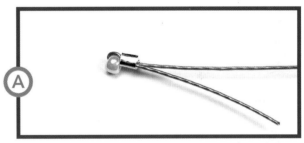

2. String three chips, a rondelle, three chips, a pearl, three chips, a rondelle, and three chips.

3. String the art bead. String three chips, a pearl, three chips, and a rondelle. Repeat twice. End with three chips.

D

4. Bring the wire back through the art bead. Alternate three chips with a pearl or rondelle as desired, until the second dangle is approximately twice as long as the first. Finish the end as in step 1.

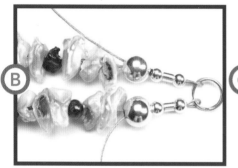

B

4. Remove the tape from the end of one wire and string an accent bead, round spacer, crimp bead, spacer, and a split ring. Go back through the beads just strung. Do not crimp the crimp bead. Repeat on the second strand, using the same split ring. Repeat on the other ends with the remaining split ring. Tighten the wires and check the fit. Add or remove an equal number of beads from each end if necessary. Crimp the crimp beads and trim the excess wire.

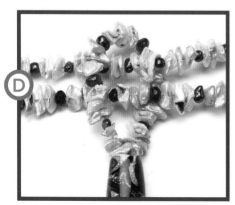

D

6. To wear the pendant, string the beaded loop over both strands. ❖

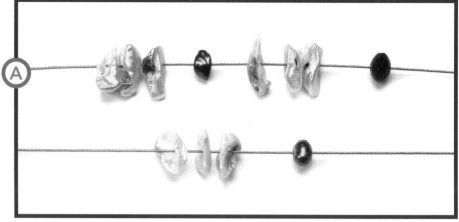

A

necklace • 1. Determine the finished length of your necklace. (These are 20 in./ 51cm.) Add 6 in. (15cm) and cut two pieces of beading wire to that length.

2. On one wire, string three chips, a pearl, three chips, and a rondelle. Repeat until the strand is within 2 in. (5cm) of the desired length. Tape the ends and set aside.

3. On the remaining wire, string three chips and a pearl. Repeat until the strand is within 2 in. of the desired length. Tape the ends and set aside.

C

5. Attach a clasp half to each split ring.

SupplyList

- 34-39mm art bead (Suzanne Leberman, sleberman@wi.rr.com)
- 3 16-in. (41cm) strands gemstone or mother-of-pearl chips
- **63-75** 2-3mm button or potato pearls
- **16-30** 2-3mm rondelles
- 4 6mm accent beads
- 2 size 11º seed beads or 3mm glass beads
- 8 2.5mm round silver spacers
- 2 6mm split rings
- flexible beading wire, .014 or .015
- 6 crimp beads
- toggle clasp
- crimping pliers
- diagonal wire cutters
- split-ring pliers (optional)

Contact Rupa at rupa@rupab.com or visit her website, rupab.com.

by Naomi Fujimoto

Garnets and gold

Quickly connect gemstone links into a bracelet

A perfect way to showcase your birthstone, this bracelet features garnets set in gold vermeil links. To mimic the coil pattern framing the gemstones, include fancy jump rings and a twisted-wire toggle with garnet detail. The design elements converge in a professional-looking piece of jewelry.

1. Open a jump ring (Basic Techniques, p. 12) and string the loop on each of two jeweled links, as shown. Close the jump ring.

2. Connect links with jump rings until the row is within 1 in. (2.5cm) of the desired length.

3. Open a jump ring and string the loop half of the clasp and one of the end links. Close the jump ring.

Open a jump ring and string the toggle half of the clasp and the remaining end link. Close the jump ring. To allow the toggle more room to pivot, link two extra jump rings before attaching the toggle. Check the fit and add or remove a link, if necessary. ✤

SupplyList

• **8-12** 11 x 17mm vermeil jeweled links with garnets (Fire Mountain Gems, 800-355-2137, firemountaingems.com)
• **9-15** 6mm twisted gold-plated jump rings
• vermeil toggle clasp
• **2** pairs chainnose pliers, or chainnose and roundnose pliers

Swing
dance

Kicky dangles sway from hoop earrings • by Yvette Jones

A pair of fabulous earrings can perk up your wardrobe, put a spring in your step, and energize your mood. In this set, the hoop's curve graduates the length of the dangles, so they swing in perfect proportion. You need only select striking colors and turn a few plain loops. Put on a pair and you just might feel like dancing.

EDITOR'S TIP
To make these earrings more quickly, substitute eye pins for 28 of the 40 head pins or for the 3 ft. (91cm) of wire used in step 2.

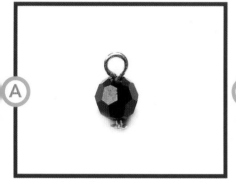

1. To make a dangle, string a round crystal on a head pin and make a plain loop (Basic Techniques, p. 12) above the bead. Make a total of six crystal dangles and set aside.

2. Trim the head from a head pin or cut a 1¼-in. (3.2cm) piece of wire. (Or, use an eye pin.) String a gemstone and make a plain loop at each end. Make a total of 14 bead units.

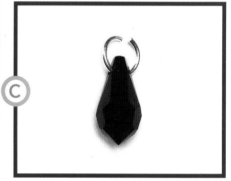

3. Open a jump ring (Basic Techniques) and string a teardrop.

4. Attach one loop of a bead unit to the jump ring and close the jump ring. Open a loop on a second bead unit and attach it to the first; close the loop. Open the top loop and attach it to the center loop on the earring hoop. Close the loop.

5. Link two bead units and a round crystal dangle by opening and closing the loops. Attach the completed dangle to an earring loop.

6. Repeat step 5 with the remaining crystals and bead units. Make a second earring to match the first. ❖

SupplyList

- **28** 4mm or 5mm round gemstones
- **12** 4mm round crystals
- **2** 11 x 5.5mm top-drilled crystal teardrops
- **40** 1½-in. (3.8cm) head pins or **12** head pins and 3 ft. (91cm) 24-gauge wire
- **2** 5mm jump rings
- pair of hoop earrings with 7 hanging loops, 25-30mm
- chainnose and roundnose pliers
- diagonal wire cutters

Contact Yvette at Chic Designs by Yvette, (914) 450-3046 or ymaddux@juno.com.

Rock
of ages

String natural stone on suede for a quick and organic necklace

by Naomi Fujimoto

Put together your own fresh necklace with a little slice of nature. Polished to perfection, geode slices are one-of-a-kind rocks with layers of crystallized minerals inside. You need not be a rock hound, however, to appreciate their beautiful bands and translucency. For an unfettered look, string a geode on a yard or so of suede, wrap around your neck, and tie a square knot. Now that's natural beauty.

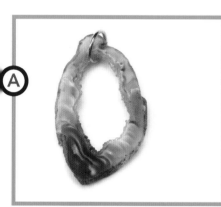

1. Open a 9mm jump ring (Basic Techniques, p. 12) and string the geode. Close the jump ring, being careful not to break the geode.

2. Determine the finished length of your necklace. (Here, the strand with the geode is 14 in./35.6cm; each of the two remaining strands is 10¼ in./26cm, which leaves enough length to knot the ends.) Cut one piece of suede cord to the longer length and two to the shorter length, allowing ¾ in. (2cm) for finishing. Center the geode pendant on the longer cord.

3. Attach a crimp end (Basic Techniques) to each end of the pendant's cord.

SupplyList

- geode, approx. 25 x 35mm (Planet Bead, 800-889-4365)
- **4** 6-8mm washers, with holes large enough to accommodate suede cord
- 3-4 ft. (.9-1.2m) suede cord, 3mm wide (Rupa Balachandar, rupab.com)
- **4** 4mm crimp ends (Fire Mountain Gems, 800-355-2137, firemountaingems.com)
- 9mm or larger jump ring, to accommodate geode
- lobster claw clasp and **2** 6mm jump rings
- chainnose and roundnose pliers or **2** pairs of chainnose pliers
- diagonal wire cutters
- E6000 adhesive

4. On one end of each of the remaining cords, attach a crimp end.

Open a 6mm jump ring and string one end loop of the pendant strand, the loop of a remaining strand, and the clasp. Close the jump ring. Repeat on the other end, omitting the clasp.

5. String two washers on each of the remaining cord ends. Make an overhand knot (Basic Techniques) on each. Check the fit, and trim any excess suede from the knotted ends, if necessary. ❧

by Brenda Schweder

You've seen them everywhere – on sweaters, jackets, scarves, and handbags. So don't be shy about "brooching" the subject; make the season's hottest accessory your own. The key finding, an ingenious pin back with a mesh dome, awaits adornment with teardrop-shaped gemstones. Add copper leaf stampings for a beautiful backdrop, bejewel the center of the pin, and the resulting look is anything but a fragile flower.

Brooch approach

Create a lovely gemstone flower pin

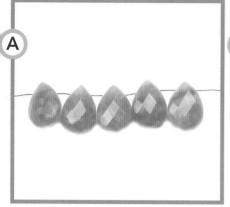

A

1. Cut an 18-in. (46cm) piece of craft wire. Center five teardrop-shaped beads on the wire.

B

2. Pass one end of the wire through the beads once more. Pull each wire end to form a flower shape.

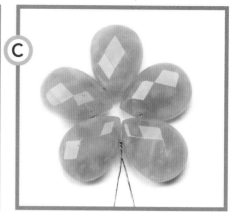

C

3. Twist the wires together three or four times.

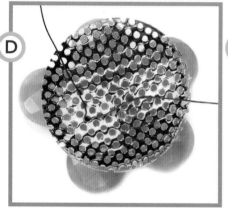

D

4. Remove the mesh dome from a pin back; set aside the pin back. Center the flower on the curved side of the dome. Pass the wires through one of the holes.

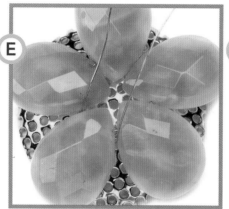

E

5. Separate the wires. Bring each end through a hole in the dome between two gemstones.

F

6. Pass each wire through another hole in the dome. Weave the wire between each gemstone.

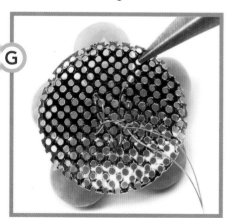

G

7. Twist the wire ends together three or four times and trim the excess wire.

8. Cut a 16-in. (41cm) piece of craft wire. String a leaf 1 in. (2.5cm) from the end and twist the shorter wire around the stem. Trim the excess wire.

Supply^{List}

both projects
- 28-gauge copper craft wire
- chainnose pliers
- diagonal wire cutters

yellow turquoise brooch
- **5** 18 x 23mm top-drilled teardrop-shaped gemstone beads, yellow turquoise
- **5** 13 x 18mm copper leaf stampings
- **5-10** 4mm rutilated quartz rondelles
- **10-15** 3mm round onyx beads
- 1¼-in. (3cm) pin back with mesh dome (Designer's Findings, 262-574-1324)
- **5-10** 1½-in. (3.8cm) brass ball-end head pins (Rio Grande, 800-545-6566, riogrande.com)

aquamarine brooch
- **5** 13 x 18mm top-drilled briolettes, synthetic aquamarine
- **5** 13 x 18mm copper leaf stampings
- **5-10** 4mm glass rondelles
- **10-15** 3mm beads (gemstone rounds and bicone crystals)
- 1¼-in. pin back with mesh dome
- **5-10** 1½-in. brass plain or ball-end head pins

9. Place the leaf between two gemstones and pass the wire through a hole in the dome. Bring the wire up and through the dome once more.

10. Bring the wire up through an adjacent pair of gemstones. String a leaf and tack down as before. Repeat to attach the three remaining leaves. Wrap the end around the core of wires on the back of the dome and trim the excess.

11. String two or three rounds, bicones, or rondelles on a head pin. String the head pin through the center of the dome. String beads on another head pin and go through another hole in the dome. Twist the head pins together, bend the wire against the dome, and trim the excess. Repeat with pairs of head pins, until the center is covered.

12. Place the dome in the pin back, positioning it as desired. Gently bend the prongs down around the dome. ✤

Brenda offers the yellow turquoise brooch as a kit. Contact her at Miss Cellany Jewelry Kits, b@brendaschweder.com, or visit brendaschweder.com.

Shortcuts

Readers' tips to make your beading life easier

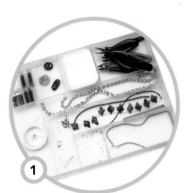

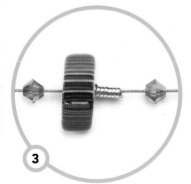

1 utensil tray

Use a wood or plastic utensil tray to organize materials and projects. The compartments are the ideal size for storing beads, findings, and tools; longer sections work well for bead strands or unfinished projects. Sturdy and portable, the tray will help you see project options at a glance.
– C. Atkins, via e-mail

2 home, sweet home

Home decorating magazines are a great source of jewelry design inspiration since they present patterns, textures, and colors in unexpected ways. Try international magazines, too – they'll lend ideas for jewelry with an ethnic flair.
– M. Rae Smith, Wauwatosa, WI

3 furnace glass bead solution

When stringing a large-hole furnace glass bead, string a wire coil to nestle inside the bead's hole. Make coils by wrapping 24-gauge wire around an 18- or 20-gauge wire. Remove the coiled wire and cut it to fit within the bead. The coils prevent smaller beads from becoming lodged inside the furnace glass.
– Veronica Stewart, via e-mail

4 vintage breakdown

Even though it's best to shop for vintage jewelry in pristine condition, don't pass up a beautiful piece because it's broken. Consider reusing the beads and the clasp in separate projects: Augment a necklace or bracelet with a pendant or new crystals, or create an entirely different piece with a vintage clasp.
– Marie Schalk, Alexander, AR

5 consistent loops

With a permanent marker, indicate on your roundnosepliers where you wrap wire loops. Use the mark as a gauge to help make the size of plain or wrapped loops consistent. If necessary, the mark can be removed with rubbing alcohol.
– R. Davis, Cleveland, OH

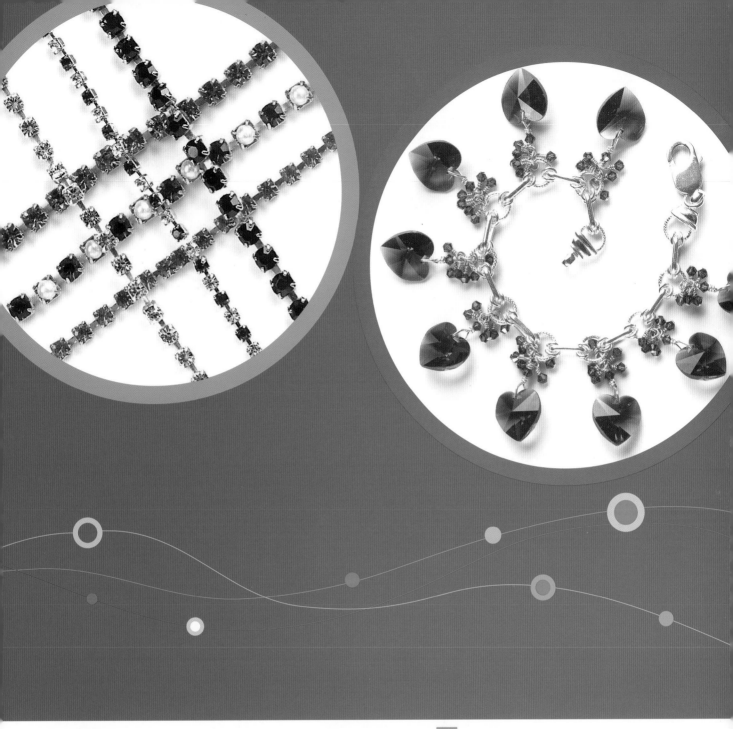

Crystals

In full

Crystal flowers catch the light in a garland-like bracelet • by Irina Miech

Reminiscent of clip-on earrings from grandma's jewelry box, these components blossom in eye-popping hues. String coordinating crystals to intensify the brilliance of this blooming arrangement. Turn these fabulous flashbacks into a fresh bracelet!

EDITOR'S TIP
Choose 6mm crystals in coordinating or contrasting colors. For maximum shine, choose two different finishes, AB and plain.

SupplyList

- **4–6** 21mm Swarovski bezel-set flower components (Eclectica, 262-641-0910, eclecticabeads.com)
- **10–14** 6mm round crystals, in AB and plain finishes
- **20–28** 4mm flat spacer beads
- 1g size 11° Japanese cylinder beads
- **6** 2mm or 3mm large-hole round spacer beads
- flexible beading wire, .014 or .015
- **2** crimp beads
- toggle clasp
- chainnose or crimping pliers
- diagonal wire cutters

A **1.** Determine the finished length of your bracelet, add 5 in. (13cm), and cut two pieces of beading wire to that length.

Center a flower on both wires, passing each wire through two holes.

B **2.** On the top strand – on one side of the flower – string three seed beads, a spacer, an AB crystal, a spacer, and six seed beads. Repeat this pattern – on the opposite side of the flower – on the bottom strand. On the remaining strands, string the pattern in reverse, substituting a plain crystal for the AB.

C **3.** On each end, string a flower on both wires. Repeat steps 2 and 3, alternating AB and plain crystals, until each strand is within 1 in. (2.5cm) of the desired length.

Irina offers the pink bracelet as a kit. Contact her at Eclectica, (262) 641-0910 or info@eclecticabeads.com.

D **4.** On one end of each strand, string a round spacer. Over both wires, string a crimp bead, a round spacer, and half the clasp. Go back through the beads just strung and tighten the wires.

Repeat on the other end. Check the fit, and add or remove beads from each end, if necessary. Crimp the crimp beads (Basic Techniques, p. 12) and trim the excess wire. ❖

bloom

by Karin Buckingham

This tiny beading chain can be used to
create an illusion style necklace or as a quick
alternative to stringing liquid silver. Be
adventurous with the earrings – this chain
is the perfect medium for long and
lean shoulder-duster dangles.

Light and lively

Make a lightweight silver and crystal necklace with matching earrings

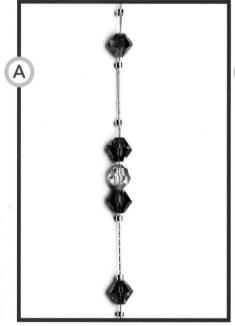

(A)

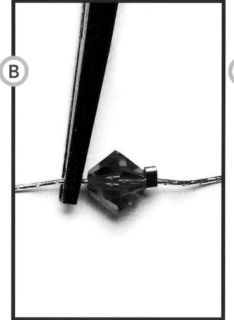

(B)

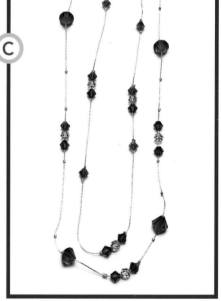

(C)

necklace • **1.** Determine the finished length of your necklace. (The shortest strand in this necklace is 16 in./.41m.) Cut a piece of beading chain to that length, and two more, each 2 in. (51mm) longer than the previous chain.

String a micro crimp, 1 to 3 crystals, and a micro crimp on the shortest strand. Continue stringing sets of crystals with micro crimps on either side.

2. Space each grouping as desired and flatten each crimp bead (Basic Techniques, p. 12).

3. Plan your second strand by staggering the placement of the crystals in comparison with the first strand. Flatten the crimp beads. Repeat for the third strand.

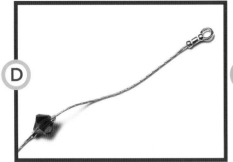

D

4. Slide a crimp-end loop onto one end of one chain. Flatten the middle crimp section with chainnose pliers. Repeat on both ends of each piece of chain.

E

5. Open a jump ring (Basic Techniques) and slide on the clasp and three crimp-end loops. Close the jump ring. Repeat on the other end with just the crimp ends.

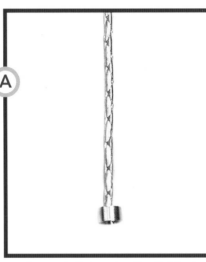

A

earrings • 1. Determine the finished length of your earrings. (These are 1½ in./ 38mm.) Cut a piece of beading chain to that length. String a micro crimp. Flatten the crimp bead at the end of the chain.

SupplyList

necklace
- 5 ft. (1.5m) beading chain, 0.6mm (Fire Mountain Gems, 800-355-2137, firemountaingems.com)
- **4** or more 10mm bicone crystals
- **33** or more 6mm bicone crystals, two colors
- **11** or more 6mm round crystals
- **50** or more micro crimps
- **6** crimp ends (loop style), 0.8mm (Fire Mountain Gems)
- **2** 4-5mm jump rings
- lobster claw clasp with jump ring
- chainnose pliers
- diagonal wire cutters

earrings
- 3 in. (76mm) or more beading chain, 0.6mm
- crystals left over from necklace
- **2** crimp ends (loop style), 0.8mm
- **2** micro crimps
- pair of earring wires
- chainnose pliers
- diagonal wire cutters

B

2. String crystals as desired.

Contact Karin in care of BeadStyle.

C

3. Slide a crimp-end loop onto the other end of the chain. Flatten the middle section with chainnose pliers.

D

4. Open the end of an earring wire and slide on the crimp-end loop. Close the earring wire. Make a second earring to match the first. ❖

If you love chandelier earrings but think they're just a little overpowering for everyday wear, here's a smaller pair of earrings you can wear with just about any outfit. These compact clusters accent casual as well as nighttime wear and still have plenty of movement and dazzle.

Shimmering
clusters

Accent casual or evening wear with compact cluster earrings

• by Lea Nowicki

1. On each of five head pins, string one of the following bead patterns: a 4mm round, a crystal, and a 4mm round; a 4mm round and a crystal; a crystal and a 4mm round; one 4mm round; one crystal. Make a plain loop (Basic Techniques, p. 12) above each bead. Make a second set.

2. To make the earring's main bead unit, cut two 3-in. (7.6cm) pieces of wire.

Make a plain loop at one end of a piece of wire. String a 6 or an 8mm bead on the wire and make a wrapped loop (Basic Techniques) above the bead. Make a second bead unit.

3. Open the bottom loop of a bead unit and attach the dangles as follows: one bead, two beads, three beads, two beads, and one bead. Close the loop.

4. Open the loop of an earring wire and attach the bead unit. Close the loop.

5. Repeat steps 3 and 4 to make a second earring. ❖

SupplyList

- 2 6 or 8mm round beads
- 8 4mm bicone crystals
- 10 4mm round beads
- 10 1½-in. (3.8cm) head pins
- 6 in. (15cm) 22-gauge wire
- pair of earring wires
- chainnose and roundnose pliers
- diagonal wire cutters

Contact Lea in care of BeadStyle.

Putting on the glitz

Rhinestone components and crystals form stunning, two-strand bracelets

by Jan Kostura

Whip up fabulous bracelets with only two basic techniques – connecting rhinestones with jump rings and turning plain loops next to crystals. If you vary component sizes, use jump rings that are slightly smaller than the crystals you're stringing. Whether your bracelet is bold and bright or subtly sparkling, you'll see that glamour can be uncomplicated.

A

purple bracelet • 1. Open a round jump ring (Basic Techniques, p. 12). Slide on two rhinestone components and close the jump ring. Use jump rings to link a total of eight rhinestone components. Repeat to link a second row of eight components. Each row should be within 1 in. (2.5cm) of the desired bracelet length; add or remove components on each row, if necessary.

B

2. Snip the heads off seven 2-in. (5cm) head pins. Make a plain loop (Basic Techniques) at one end of each to form an eye pin.

3. String a blue crystal on one eye pin. Go through the first jump ring, as shown.

C

4. String two yellow crystals, then go through the first jump ring of the second row of components.

5. String a blue crystal and make a plain loop ⅛ in. (3mm) above the bead. (The extra space ensures flexibility in the bracelet.)

D

E

6. Link the next two rhinestone sections using green/pink and blue/light blue crystals as shown. Alternate the blue and green sections. Repeat with the remaining crystals and head pins until you have connected all seven pairs of jump rings.

7. String a 7mm purple crystal on a ⅞-in. (2.2cm) head pin and make a plain loop above the bead. Make a total of 14 dangles.

F

8. Open the loops on the dangles and attach them to the ends of each vertical crystal section. Close the loops.

G

9. Open two oval jump rings. String each through a rhinestone component and a clasp loop. Close the jump rings. Repeat on the other end with the remaining clasp half.

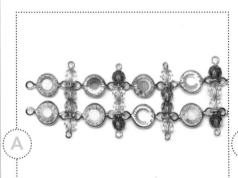

A

B

clear bracelet • 1. Connect 11 channels with jump rings, as in step 1 of the purple bracelet. Repeat to make a second row. Adjust the fit as necessary.

2. Snip the heads off ten 1½-in. (3.8cm) head pins. Make a plain loop at the end of each.

String crystal combinations of light blue/aqua and light blue/gray as in steps 3 through 5 of the purple bracelet, alternating with olive/yellow crystals. Repeat until you have connected all ten pairs of jump rings.

3. String a brown crystal on a ⅞-in. head pin and make a plain loop above the bead. Make a total of 20 dangles, then attach each dangle as in step 8.

4. Attach the clasp as in step 9, substituting 3mm round jump rings for the oval jump rings. ❖

Jan offers kits for the purple bracelet. Contact her at Jan's Jewels and More, (405) 840-2341, jan@jansjewels.com, or visit jansjewels.com.

3. Open another jump ring. Link it through the previous jump ring, between the two dangles. String two dangles on the jump ring and close it.

4. Repeat step 3 twice.

D

5. Open a jump ring. Link it through the previous jump ring, between the two dangles, and close it. Open another jump ring and string a dangle. Link it through the previous jump ring and close it. Make a second earring to match the first. ❖

Connect the drops

Suspend jewel-tone drop beads from linked jump rings for a pair of deceptively easy earrings • **by Fran Farris**

To vary the cluster's shape, use a smaller or larger jump ring – 4mm for a short, full earring or 5mm for a long, narrow dangle. After assembling your first pair, you won't even need the instructions.

Supply List

- **18** 5 x 7mm Czech fire-polished crystal drop beads (Shipwreck Beads, 800-950-4232, shipwreckbeads.com)
- **18** 1½-in. (3.8cm) head pins
- **12** 4mm or 5mm jump rings
- pair of lever-back earrings
- chainnose and roundnose pliers
- diagonal wire cutters

Contact Fran at ffarris@wcta.net.

A

1. String a crystal on a head pin and make a wrapped loop (Basic Techniques, p. 12). Make 18 dangles.

B

2. Open a jump ring (Basic Techniques). String an earring's loop and two dangles on the jump ring and close it.

Suspend glass hearts from classic chain for a charming bracelet

Heart of glass

by Nancy Kugel

Whether you choose hearts in a single shade or several colors, a plain chain bracelet can create a stylish setting for showing your sentiment. The delicate grouping of crystals in this bracelet not only adds sparkle, but also provides an ingenious showcase for your wrapped-loop workmanship. So think of someone close to your heart, choose a color scheme, start making loops, and put together a special gift.

EDITOR'S TIP
Substituting plain loops for wrapped loops creates an equally stunning bracelet in less time.

SupplyList

bracelet
- **9** 14 x 14mm crystal heart pendants (Rings & Things, 800-366-2156, rings-things.com)
- **63** 3mm bicone crystals, **7** for each heart
- 6.8mm chain link bracelet (Rio Grande, 800-545-6566)
- **30** in. (76cm) 22-gauge sterling silver wire, half hard
- **54** 1-in. (2.5cm) 24-gauge head pins

- chainnose and roundnose pliers
- diagonal wire cutters

earrings
- **2** 10 x 10mm crystal heart pendants
- **8** 3mm bicone crystals
- **6** in. (15cm) 22-gauge sterling silver wire, half hard
- **6** 1-in. 24-gauge head pins
- pair of earring wires
- chainnose and roundnose pliers
- diagonal wire cutters

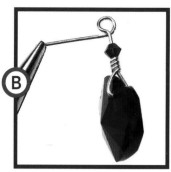

bracelet • 1. String a bicone crystal on a head pin and make a wrapped loop (Basic Techniques, p. 12) above the crystal. Make six dangles for each heart.

2. Cut a 3-in. (7.6cm) piece of wire. Center the heart on the wire and make two or three wraps above it (Basic Techniques). Trim the wraps' excess wire. String a bicone crystal. Make the first half of a wrapped loop.

3. String six dangles on the top loop.
  Repeat steps 2 and 3 with the remaining hearts.

4. Find the center link of the bracelet and attach a heart unit to the link. Complete the wraps.

5. Continue attaching hearts at even intervals on the same side of the chain. Alternate colors if using more than one.

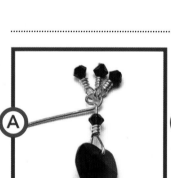

earrings • 1. Make three dangles as in step 1 of the bracelet. Substitute a 10mm heart for the 14mm heart and repeat step 2 of the bracelet. Attach the dangles to the loop and complete the wraps.

2. Open the loop on an earring wire and attach the heart dangle. Close the earring's loop. Make a second earring to match the first. ❖

Nancy offers kits for this project. Contact her at engeekay@sbcglobal.net or www.engee-kay.com.

Holiday style

Design a festive crystal necklace and bracelet

by Tracy Bretl

Even the perfect outfit will lack style without the perfect accessories. That's where the fun comes in for beaders. Often making jewelry to match a specific outfit results in a sparkling favorite.

Crystal shapes and sizes can dictate design. In this case, an asymmetrical pattern was the best way to accentuate the wide variety of crystals used here.

Make your own version by following some simple design guidelines:

- Work in sets of three crystals for the background pattern; separate sets with a Japanese cylinder bead for added dimension.
- Keep the shapes the same in a set, but alternate sizes or colors.
- Create accents by separating the strands and stringing flowers in different sizes and shapes.
- Use a design board to help you plan.
- Enjoy the creative journey!

The instructions below illustrate how to string flowers you can incorporate in a necklace or bracelet. Make small flowers with 3mm bicones, 4mm bicones, 4mm rounds, 6mm rounds, or 6mm bicones surrounding an 8mm accent bicone. Large flowers use 8mm rounds.

small flower • 1. When you're ready to begin your flower, string a cylinder bead over two wires. Separate the wires and string a cylinder bead, a main color crystal, and a cylinder bead on each.

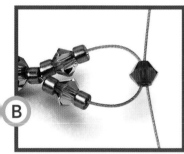

2. Cross both wires through an accent color crystal.

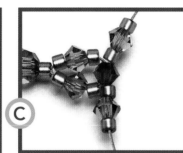

3. String a cylinder bead, a main color crystal, and a cylinder bead on each strand.

4. String both wires through a cylinder bead. This completes a small flower.

large flower • Follow the steps for the small flower, but use 8mm crystals separated by two cylinder beads, as shown.

 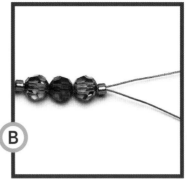 

A B C

necklace • **1.** Determine the finished length of your necklace. (This one is 23 in./ 58cm.) Add 6 in. (15cm) and cut two pieces of beading wire to that length. Over both wires, string a cylinder bead, crimp bead, cylinder bead, and half the clasp. Go back through the beads just strung and tighten the wires. Crimp the crimp bead (Basic Techniques, p. 12).

2. Begin the background pattern by stringing a cylinder bead, three crystals, and a cylinder bead over both wires, hiding the wire tails. Use any combination of 3 or 4mm crystals, keeping the design tips (see p. 180) in mind.

3. String a small flower (see p. 181 for instructions).

D

4. Continue stringing the background pattern, alternating sizes, shapes, and colors of crystals, as desired. Separate each set of three crystals with a cylinder bead. Add flowers in a variety of sizes throughout the necklace. This necklace has nine small flowers and one large flower.

5. When you are about ½ in. (1.3cm) from the desired length, check the fit and add or remove crystals, if necessary. Attach the remaining clasp half as in step 1.

Supply List

Swarovski crystals in olivine and light Siam comprise the holly version; Indian sapphire and fuchsia are an alternate combination.

Crystal quantities will vary.

necklace
main color crystals
- **5** 8mm rounds
- **12** 6mm rounds
- **16** 6mm bicones
- **28** 4mm rounds
- **33** 4mm bicones
- **18** 3mm bicones

accent color crystals
- **1** 8mm round
- **4** 8mm bicones
- **5** 6mm rounds
- **6** 4mm rounds
- **6** 4mm bicones
- **1** 3mm bicone
- 2g size 11º Japanese cylinder beads to match main color
- flexible beading wire, .010 or .012
- **2** crimp beads
- clasp
- chainnose or crimping pliers
- diagonal wire cutters

bracelet
main color crystals
- **3** 6mm rounds
- **7** 6mm bicones
- **8** 4mm rounds
- **10** 4mm bicones
- **4** 3mm bicones

accent color crystals
- **1** 8mm round
- **2** 8mm bicones
- **1** 6mm round
- **1** 4mm round
- **2** 4mm bicones
- 1g size 11º Japanese cylinder beads to match main color
- flexible beading wire, .010 or .012
- **2** crimp beads
- clasp
- chainnose or crimping pliers
- diagonal wire cutters

Contact Tracy in care of BeadStyle.

(A)

bracelet • 1. Determine the finished length of your bracelet. Add 5 in. (13cm) and cut two pieces of beading wire to that length.

2. Over both wires, string a cylinder bead, three crystals, and a cylinder bead. Repeat with different crystals. String a flower (see p. 181). Repeat until the bracelet is 1 in. shorter than the desired length. Vary the sizes and shapes of the crystals and the flowers; end with a crystal pattern.

(B)

3. On each end, attach a clasp half as in step 1 of the necklace. Tighten the wires and check the fit. Add or remove beads, if necessary. Crimp the crimp beads and trim the excess wire. ✤

by Karen Woodson

Spectacular jewelry adds the perfect touch to special-occasion dressing. A dress with a graceful neckline, a stylish updo, and stunning accessories add up to a sophisticated, show-stopping ensemble. This set has plenty of sparkle, and the clean lines of the cubes and squares provide added elegance. Be the belle of the ball with your favorite little black dress and this brilliant crystal creation.

Glamour

Cubes and squares distinguish this lavish necklace, bracelet, and earring set

A

B

C

necklace • 1. Determine the finished length of your necklace. (This one is 15 in./38cm.) Add 10 in. (25cm) and cut a piece of beading wire to that length.

Center a 2mm round on the wire. Bring the ends together and string a 6mm light saucer, an 8mm squaredelle, an 8mm cube, an 8mm squaredelle, a 6mm saucer, and a 2mm round over both ends.

2. Slide the beads down to the centered 2mm round. Separate the wires, and string a 3mm crystal on each end.

3. On each end, string a 5mm light saucer, a 6mm squaredelle, a 6mm cube, a 6mm squaredelle, and a 5mm light saucer.

girl

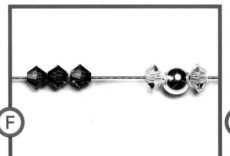

4. String a 5mm round, a 5mm dark saucer, and a 5mm round. Repeat on the other end.

5. Repeat steps 3 and 4 once, on each end.

6. On each end, string a 5mm light saucer, a 4mm squaredelle, a 4mm cube, a 4mm squaredelle, a 5mm light saucer, and a 5mm round bead.

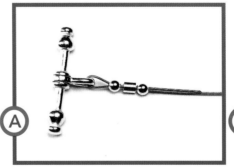

7. *Blue necklace*: On each end, string three 4mm bicones, a 5mm light saucer, a 5mm round, and a light saucer. Repeat until the necklace is within 1 in. (2.5cm) of the desired length, ending with three bicones.

Black necklace: On each end, string three 4mm bicones, a 5mm dark saucer, a 5mm round, and a dark saucer. Repeat until the necklace is within 1 in. of the desired length, ending with three bicones.

8. String a 2mm round, a crimp bead, a 2mm round, and half the clasp. Go back through the beads just strung and tighten the wire. Repeat on the other end. Check the fit, and add or remove an equal number of bicones from each end, if necessary. Crimp the crimp beads (Basic Techniques, p. 12) and trim the excess wire.

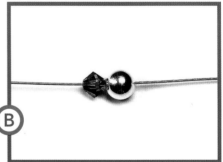

bracelet • 1. Determine the finished length of your bracelet, add 5 in. (13cm), and cut a piece of beading wire to that length. String a 2mm round, a crimp bead, a 2mm round, and half the clasp. Go back through the beads just strung and tighten the wire, but do not crimp the crimp bead.

2. String a 4mm bicone and a 5mm round.

3. String a light saucer, a squaredelle, a cube, a squaredelle, a crystal saucer, a round, a dark saucer, and a round. Repeat this pattern until the bracelet is within 1 in. of the desired length (omit the last round bead).

Attach the other clasp half as in step 1. Check the fit, and add or remove beads from each end, if necessary. Crimp the crimp beads and trim the excess wire.

4. String a light saucer, a squaredelle, a cube, a squaredelle, and a saucer on a head pin. Make the first half of a wrapped loop (Basic Techniques) above the top bead.

5. Slide the dangle onto the loop end of the clasp and complete the wraps.

earrings • **1.** String a light saucer, a squaredelle, a cube, a squaredelle, and a light saucer on a head pin. Make the first half of a wrapped loop above the top bead.

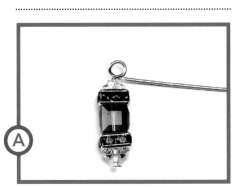

2. Slide the dangle onto the earring finding's loop and complete the wraps. Make a second earring to match the first. ❖

Karen offers kits in several colors. Contact her at Too Cute Beads, (248) 888-9925 or visit toocutebeads.com.

Chill with

Faceted dangles lend motion to a bracelet and earrings

Let this shimmery, shimmying set do all the work while you sit back and chill. Combine sherbety orange with muted pinks and peaches, or pale green with soft teals and aquas. The sparkling finishes and substantial width are ideal for a gal on the go, or for someone just watching the world go by.

crystals

by Molli Schultz

bracelet • **1.** For each dangle, open a 3mm jump ring (Basic Techniques, p. 12) and string a saucer and a 2mm jump ring. Close the jump ring. Make a total of 25 dangles. Set one aside for the chain extender in step 6.

2. Determine the finished length of your bracelet, add 5 in. (13cm), and cut five pieces of beading wire to that length. On each wire, center 10–12 crystals interspersed with one or two dangles. String the lightest colored crystals on the outside strands, the darkest on the second and fourth strands, and the remaining crystals on the middle strand.

bracelet

- **25–28** 6mm or 9mm crystal saucers, top drilled (Eclectica, 262-641-0910, eclecticabeads.com)
- **5** 8-in. (20cm) strands 4mm Czech fire-polished crystals: **2** strands each of two colors and **1** strand of a third color
- **27–30** 3mm jump rings
- **25–28** 2mm jump rings
- **2** five-strand spacer bars
- **20** 3mm round spacer beads
- flexible beading wire, .014 or .015
- **10** crimp beads
- **2** five-to-one connector bars
- lobster claw clasp
- 1½-2 in. (3.8-5cm) chain, 5mm links
- chainnose and roundnose pliers or **2** pairs of chainnose pliers
- diagonal wire cutters
- crimping pliers (optional)

earrings

- **2** 6mm or 9mm crystal saucers, top drilled (Eclectica)
- **2** 3mm jump rings
- **18** 4mm Czech fire-polished crystals, **8** each of two colors and **2** of the third color, leftover from the bracelet
- **10** 1½-in. decorative head pins
- 15 in. (38cm) 1.5mm fine chain
- **2** five-to-one connector bars
- pair of decorative earring wires
- chainnose and roundnose pliers
- diagonal wire cutters

EDITOR'S TIP

You may use 3mm, 4mm, 5mm, or 6mm Czech fire-polished crystals, but use a consistent size throughout the bracelet. Mixing sizes will result in uneven strand lengths.

3. On each end of each wire, string the respective hole of a spacer bar. String crystals and dangles as in step 2, until the bracelet is within 2 in. (5cm) of the finished length.

4. On each end of each wire, string a round spacer, crimp bead, round spacer, and the respective loop of a clasp half. Go back through the beads just strung and tighten the wires. Check the fit, and add or remove beads from each end if necessary. Crimp the crimp beads (Basic Techniques) and trim the excess wire.

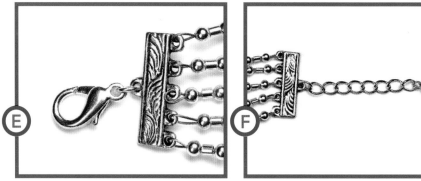

5. Open a 3mm jump ring. On one end, string the lobster claw clasp and the remaining loop of a connector bar. Close the jump ring.

6. Open a 3mm jump ring. String an end link of chain and the other connector bar's remaining loop. Close the jump ring.

Open the extra dangle's 3mm jump ring and attach it to the other end link of chain. Close the jump ring.

earrings • 1. Cut five pieces of chain: one 2¾, two 2¼, and two 2 in. (7, 5.7, and 5cm, respectively).

Open a 3mm jump ring and string a saucer and an end link of the longest chain. Close the jump ring.

2. String a crystal on a 1½-in. (3.8cm) decorative head pin and make a plain loop (Basic Techniques) above the crystal. (Set aside the remaining part of the head pin's wire for step 4.) String a total of four dangles in two colors.

3. Open the loop of a dangle and string an end link of chain. Close the loop. Repeat with each of the three remaining dangles and chain pieces, matching crystal colors on the chains.

4. String a crystal on a wire (from step 2). Make a plain loop at each end. Make a total of four dangles in the two colors used in step 2. Trim the head from a head pin and make a fifth dangle with the third-color crystal.

5. Open the loop of the fifth crystal dangle and string the remaining end link of the longest chain. Close the loop. Repeat with each of the remaining dangles and chain pieces, matching crystal colors with chain lengths.

Contact Molli in care of BeadStyle.

6. Open the loop above the crystal on the longest chain and string the center loop of the connector bar. Close the loop. Repeat with each of the remaining chain pieces, attaching the shortest lengths of chain to the outer loops of the connector bar.

Open the loop on an earring wire and string the remaining loop of the connector bar. Close the loop. Make a second earring to match the first. ❖

by Jane Konkel

Perhaps you possess the supreme bohemian within. What better way to express this inclination than with a pair of unconventional earrings? Like an artist exploring different media, you can mix various materials, lengths, and color combinations. Be thrifty and incorporate leftover bits of chain into your clever creations, and reveal your inner artist.

Gypsy jewels

Crystals drift from chains in distinctive earrings

A

1. Cut a 2½-in. (6.4cm) length of wire. String two crystals, a saturn bead, and two crystals, alternating crystal colors.

2. Make the first half of a wrapped loop on each end (Basic Techniques, p. 12).

B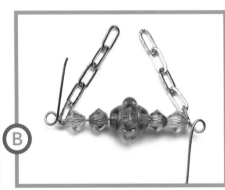

3. Cut two ¾-in. (2cm) segments of fine chain. String one end link through one end of the wire, positioning it against the outside crystal. Repeat on the other end of the wire with the remaining piece of chain.

C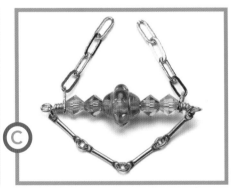

4. Cut a 1½-in. (3.8cm) segment of medium chain, making sure there is a round link in the center. Attach each end link of chain to a loop and complete the wraps.

Supply List

- **2** 9 x 6mm oval crystals
- **2** 8mm Czech glass saturn beads (Rio Grande, 800-545-6566, riogrande.com)
- **16** 4mm bicone crystals, **8** each of 2 colors
- **5** in. (13cm) 24-gauge wire
- **4** in. (10cm) each of 2 chains, 1 fine and 1 medium (see options, below)
- **10** 1½-in. (3.8cm) plain or decorative head pins
- **2-4** 4mm jump rings
- pair of earring wires
- roundnose and chainnose pliers
- diagonal wire cutters

EDITOR'S TIP

For earrings that hang perpendicular to your ear lobe, rather than parallel, attach a second jump ring to the first.

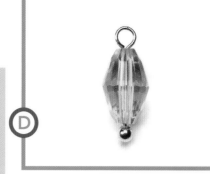

5. String an oval crystal on a decorative head pin. Make a plain loop (Basic Techniques) above the crystal. Make four more dangles with bicone crystals.

6. Open the loop of the oval dangle and attach it to the center link on the lower chain. Close the loop. Attach the remaining bicone dangles to the lower chain, alternating colors.

7. Open a jump ring (Basic Techniques) and string each end link of the upper chain. Close the jump ring.

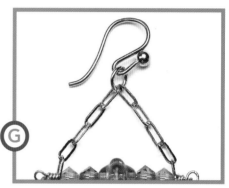

8. Open an earring wire's loop. String the jump ring. Close the loop. Make a second earring to match the first. ✤

OPTIONS					
fine chain	2.5mm flat drawn cable, brass	1.6mm triple long-and-short, gold filled	1.5mm rolo, sterling silver	2.5mm flat drawn cable, brass	1.6mm triple long-and-short, gold filled
medium chain	.9mm bar-and-link, brass	.9mm bar-and-link, brass	2.5mm rolo, sterling silver	3.6mm long-and-short, gold filled	3.6mm long-and-short, gold filled
4mm crystals	aqua erinite	emerald erinite	morion black diamond	olivine peridot	sapphire light sapphire
saturn bead	aqua	emerald	jet	peridot	sapphire
9x6mm oval	aqua AB	erinite AB	black diamond AB	chrysolite AB	sapphire AB

by Jan Kostura

Instant heirlooms

Unexpected colors accent a timeless necklace and earrings

Rose glass in scalloped settings catches plenty of light. Adding aqua crystals provides a jolt of color, and brass findings accentuate the jewelry's vintage look. This necklace and earrings look like antique-store finds; no one will guess how quickly and recently you made them.

princess-length necklace (18 in./46cm)

• **1.** String an 8mm crystal on a head pin. Make a plain loop (Basic Techniques, p. 12) above the bead. Set the dangle aside.

Trim the head from a head pin. String a 6mm crystal and make a plain loop at each end. Make a total of 22 plain loop units.

2. To make beaded chains, open the loop on a bead unit, link to another unit, and close the loop. Make three two-unit chains by linking a perpendicular unit with a plain loop unit (see Editor's Tip below).

Make two three-unit chains and two five-unit chains by linking plain loop bead units.

3. Open two 4mm jump rings (Basic Techniques). Attach a jump ring to each rhinestone component's loop. Close the jump rings. Repeat with the five remaining components.

4. To make the center section, open a jump ring on a rhinestone component. Attach a two-unit chain and close the jump ring. Attach another component to the other end of the chain.

EDITOR'S TIP

When linking an even number of bead units to make beaded chains, make sure one of the bead units has perpendicular loops, to ensure that the rhinestone components lay flat. To make a perpendicular loop, hold one bead unit's loop with chainnose pliers and twist the other loop 90 degrees with another pair of chainnose pliers.

E

F

5. On each side of the center section, attach a three-unit chain and a rhinestone component.

On each end, attach a two-unit chain and a rhinestone component, then a five-unit chain. Check the fit, and add or remove an equal number of bead units from each end if necessary.

6. Open a jump ring and string the end loop and the clasp. Close the jump ring.

Repeat on the other end of the necklace, substituting a 6mm jump ring for the clasp. Open the loop on the crystal dangle, attach it to the 6mm jump ring, and close the loop.

A

B

choker (16 in./41cm) • 1. Follow step 1 of the princess-length necklace, making one 8mm crystal dangle and a total of 20 6mm crystal plain loop units.

Make five two-unit chains and two five-unit chains, as in step 2 of the princess-length necklace.

2. Follow steps 3 and 4 of the princess-length necklace.

3. On each end, attach a two-unit chain and a rhinestone component. Repeat. Attach a five-unit chain to each end. Check the fit, and add or remove an equal number of bead units from each end if necessary.

4. Follow step 6 to finish.

Supply List

all projects
- **2 pairs of chainnose pliers**
- roundnose pliers
- diagonal wire cutters

choker or princess-length necklace (16 or 18 in./41 or 46cm)
- **6** 15 x 18mm rhinestone components
- **8mm Czech fire-polished crystal, aqua**
- **20–26** 6mm Czech fire-polished crystals, aqua
- **14** 4mm jump rings
- **6mm soldered jump ring**
- lobster claw or hook clasp
- **21–27** ⅞-in. (2.2cm) head pins

earrings
- **2** 15 x 18 rhinestone components
- **2** 8mm Czech fire-polished crystals, aqua
- **2** ⅞-in. head pins
- pair of earring wires

A

B

earrings • 1. String an 8mm crystal on a head pin and make a plain loop above the bead. Open the loop and attach it to a component's loop. Close the loop.

2. Open the loop on an earring wire and attach to the remaining loop on the component. Close the loop. Make a second earring to match the first. ❖

Jan offers kits for the necklaces and earrings. Contact her at Jan's Jewels and More, (405) 840-2341, jan@jansjewels.com, or visit jansjewels.com.

Vintage vogue

by Lauren Branca

Sparkling crystals and luminescent pearls dazzle in a four-strand necklace

With crystals reminiscent of a vintage chandelier, this striking necklace makes a bold statement. The three top strands graduate a half inch in length, lending a subtle drape to the choker portion of the piece. The longer strand boasts a faceted crystal pendant, adding a surprisingly modern twist to the choker. Try classic white pearls or pale, muted shades and create your own future heirloom.

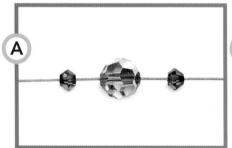

1. Determine the finished length of your necklace. (These strands are 14, 14½, 15, and 17½ in./35.6, 36.8, 38.1, and 44.5cm, respectively.) Add 6 in. (15cm) to each measurement and cut a piece of beading wire to each length.

On the shortest wire, center a bicone, a round crystal, and a bicone.

2. On each end, string three pearls, a bicone, a round crystal, and a bicone. Repeat until the strand is within 1 in. (2.5cm) of the desired length. Tape the ends.

On the second longest (the third) wire, center the pattern in step 1. Then, repeat the pattern above until the strand is within 1 in. of the desired length. Tape the ends.

3. On the shorter of the remaining wires, center the pattern in step 1.

On each end, string a pearl, a bicone, a round crystal, and a bicone. Repeat this pattern on each end until the strand is within 1 in. of the desired length. Tape the ends.

Supply List

- crystal pendant (the drop is 31 x 50mm; the round is 40mm)
- **2** 20-in. (51cm) strands 5mm round Swarovski pearls
- **60-70** 6mm round crystals
- **4mm** accent crystal (optional)
- **120-140** 3mm bicone crystals
- flexible beading wire, .014 or .015
- 4 in. (10cm) 22-gauge wire, half hard
- **16** 3mm round spacers
- **8** crimp beads
- four-strand clasp
- chainnose and roundnose pliers
- diagonal wire cutters
- crimping pliers (optional)

EDITOR'S TIP

Use man-made pearls for this project. Their consistent size will ensure an accurate pattern and fit.

4. String the pendant on the 22-gauge wire 1½ in. (3.8cm) from one end and bend each wire upward around the pendant, as in wrapping above a top-drilled bead (Basic Techniques, p. 12). Wrap the shorter wire around the longer wire and trim the excess.

5. String a 4mm or 6mm crystal and make a wrapped loop (Basic Techniques) above the bead.

6. On the remaining wire, center a bicone, the pendant, and a bicone.

7. On each end, string five pearls, a bicone, a round crystal, and a bicone. Repeat until the strand is within 1 in. of the desired length. Tape the ends.

Kits are available for the necklace on page 197. Contact Lauren at A Grain of Sand, (704) 660-3125 or suzanne@agrainofsand.com, or visit agrainofsand.com.

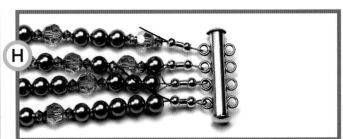

8. Remove the tape from each strand. On one end of each strand, string a round spacer, a crimp bead, a spacer, and the respective loop on half the clasp. Go back through the last beads strung and tighten the wires. Repeat on the other end. Check the fit, and add or remove an equal number of beads from each end if necessary. Crimp the crimp beads (Basic Techniques) and trim the excess wire. ❖

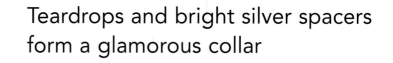

Teardrops and bright silver spacers
form a glamorous collar

Dazzling drops

by Eva Kapitany

The sparkle of cut crystal merges with the glimmer of silver spacers to create an irresistible necklace – a stunning result of the combination of only two elements. Select a rich shade of crystal, such as emerald or Montana blue, or alternate two colors for a dramatic effect. To help the crystals stay positioned in opposite directions, alternate shiny spacers with the crystals. Amazingly simple to string, this collar provides instant impact.

necklace • 1. Determine the finished length of your necklace. (This one is 15 in./38cm.) Add 6 in. (15cm) and cut a piece of beading wire to that length.

String a round spacer, rhinestone ball, crimp bead, round spacer, and jump ring. Go back through the beads just strung, tighten the wire, and crimp the crimp bead (Basic Techniques, p. 12). Trim the excess wire.

2. String an alternating pattern of flat spacers and drops until the necklace is within 1 in. (2.5cm) of the desired length. End with a spacer.

3. String a round spacer, rhinestone ball, crimp bead, spacer, and a jump ring. Go back through the beads just strung. Repeat on the other end. Tighten the wire and check the fit. Add or remove beads, if necessary. Crimp the crimp bead and trim the excess wire. If desired, close half the S-hook clasp around one jump ring with chainnose pliers.

bracelet • 1. Determine the finished length of your bracelet, add 5 in. (13cm), and cut a piece of beading wire to that length. String a bicone, round spacer, crimp bead, spacer, and half the clasp. Go back through the beads just strung, tighten the wire, and crimp the crimp bead. Trim the excess wire.

2. String beads as in step 2 of the necklace until the bracelet is within 1 in. of the desired length. Finish the bracelet as in step 1, checking the fit before crimping. ✤

Contact Eva in care of BeadStyle.

Supply^{List}

SupplyList

both projects
- flexible beading wire, .018 or .019
- chainnose or crimping pliers
- diagonal wire cutters

necklace
- **58-70** 9 x 18mm cut crystal drops (Shipwreck Beads, 800-950-4232, shipwreckbeads.com)
- **59-71** 6-7mm flat spacers
- **2** 10mm rhinestone balls, crystal (Shipwreck Beads)

- **4** 3mm round spacer beads
- **2** crimp beads
- S-hook clasp and **2** soldered jump rings

bracelet
- **23-29** 9 x 18mm cut crystal drops
- **24-30** 6-7mm flat spacers
- **2** 6mm bicone crystals (color to match drops)
- **4** 3mm round spacer beads
- **2** crimp beads
- clasp

Dramatic

Brilliant crystal earrings spice up any occasion

by Christianne Camera

A

B

C

1. String an 8mm round crystal and a cylinder bead on a head pin. Substitute a 6 x 9mm drop or oval for the 8mm round if desired. Make a wrapped loop (Basic Techniques, p. 12) above the top bead.

2. Trim the heads from six head pins. On each, make a plain loop (Basic Techniques) at one end. Or, use eye pins.
String a crystal of a different shape and/or color and a cylinder bead on an eye pin and make a wrapped loop above the top bead.

3. On another eye pin, string a crystal and a cylinder bead. Shown here is a 6 x 7mm cone, but you may substitute a 6mm round, 6mm roundelle, 4mm round, or a 4mm bicone for the cone, if desired. Make a wrapped loop above the top bead.

D

E

F

4. String a 6mm round (or a 4mm round or bicone) and a cylinder bead on an eye pin. Make a wrapped loop above the top bead.

5. Open each plain loop and attach the bead units as shown, with the head pin unit at the bottom.

6. Open the loop on an earring wire and attach the loop of the top bead unit. Close the earring wire loop. Make a second earring to match the first. ❖

dangles

Unusual crystal shapes – cones, ovals, and roundelles – add visual interest to these dangling earrings. With the wide array of colors available, you can make a pair to spruce up any outfit. The earrings are surprisingly easy to make, so whip up several pairs, to wear or give as gifts.

SupplyList

- **8 crystals; 2** each in various colors, shapes, and sizes, including:
  8mm round
  6 x 9mm oval
  5 x 7.5mm oval
  6 x 9mm drop
  6 x 7mm cone-shaped
  6mm round
  6mm rondelle
  6mm bicone
  4mm bicone
  5mm round
- **8** size 11º Japanese cylinder beads
- **8** 1½-in. (3.8cm) head pins or **6** 1½-in. eye pins and **2** 1½-in. head pins
- pair of earring wires
- chainnose and roundnose pliers
- diagonal wire cutters

Contact Christianne in care of BeadStyle.

Blend a variety of crystals into a sparkling necklace

Crystal medley

Anchored with two sparkling dangles, this single-strand necklace incorporates a variety of crystal shapes and sizes. String a necklace in one color for a classic, beautiful style, or opt for a multicolor version. Start by selecting cones and rondelles first (they're available in limited colors), and build from there. Either way, you'll have jewels that harmonize with any look.

by Tracy Bretl

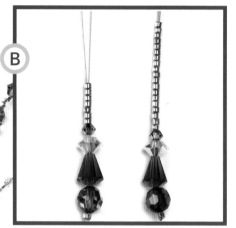

A

1. Determine the finished length of your necklace, including the dangle. (This one is 18 in./46cm plus a 2-in./5cm dangle.) Double that measurement, add 6 in. (15cm), and cut two pieces of beading wire to that length.

2. On one wire, string a Japanese cylinder bead. Center the bead and fold the wire in half.

B

3. Over both strands, string a 6mm round, a cone, a rondelle, a 3mm or 4mm bicone, and seven cylinder beads.

4. Repeat steps 2 and 3 on the remaining wire, stringing 19 cylinder beads instead of 7.

C

5. String a 6mm round over all four wires, then separate the respective pairs of wires.

SupplyList

- **2** 6.6 x 6mm cone-shaped crystals
- **9-11** 6mm round crystals
- **6-8** 6mm bicone crystals
- **2** 6mm crystal rondelles
- **14-18** 4mm round crystals
- **12-18** 4mm bicone crystals
- **18-22** 3mm bicone crystals
- 2g size 11º Japanese cylinder beads
- flexible beading wire, .010
- **2** crimp beads
- clasp
- chainnose or crimping pliers
- diagonal wire cutters

D

E

6. On one pair of wires, string five cylinder beads, a 3mm bicone, two cylinders, a 4mm round, two cylinders, a 6mm bicone, two cylinders, a 4mm round, two cylinders, and a 3mm bicone.

7. String five cylinder beads, a 4mm bicone, three cylinders, a 6mm round, three cylinders, and a 4mm bicone.

F

G

8. Repeat steps 6 and 7 two or three times. On the remaining pair of wires, follow steps 6 through 8.

9. On each end, string five cylinder beads, a 3mm bicone, three cylinders, a 4mm round, three cylinders, and a 3mm bicone. String cylinders until the necklace is within 1 in. (2.5cm) of the desired length.

10. Over each pair of wires, string a crimp bead, a cylinder bead, and half the clasp. Go back through the beads just strung plus a few more and tighten the wires. Check the fit, and add or remove an equal number of beads from each end if necessary. Crimp the crimp beads (Basic Techniques, p. 12) and trim the excess wire. ❖

Contact Tracy in care of BeadStyle.

Luxe be a lady

Discover the easy glamor of rhinestone chain
by Ellen Friedenberg

When you have an occasion to drape yourself in jewels, it doesn't get any easier than this: Purchase rhinestone chain by the foot, attach two end pieces and a clasp, and you're ready to go. It will take longer to choose your colors than to make this sparkly, ladylike set.

A

B

C

bracelet • **1.** Determine the finished length of your bracelet. Subtract the clasp measurement and cut a section of chain to that length.

2. Slide the end rhinestone into an end connector. Squeeze the sides of the end connector with chainnose pliers.

3. Using chainnose pliers, fold down the prongs on the end connector to secure the rhinestone. Repeat steps 2 and 3 on the other end.

4. On each end, attach a split ring and half the clasp.

earrings • **1.** Cut a piece of chain to the desired length of the earrings. Attach an end connector as in steps 2 and 3 of the bracelet.

2. Open the loop on an earring wire and attach the dangle. Close the loop. Make a second earring to match the first. ❖

Contact Ellen at ellenbeads@gmail.com.

Supply List

bracelet
- 1 ft. (30cm) rhinestone chain (Costume Jewelry Supplies, 434-836-0099 or costumejewelrysupplies. com)
- **2** square or round end connectors (Costume Jewelry Supplies)
- clasp
- **2** split rings
- chainnose pliers
- diagonal wire cutters
- split-ring pliers (optional)

earrings
- rhinestone chain left-over from the bracelet
- **2** round end connectors
- pair of earring wires
- chainnose pliers
- diagonal wire cutters

Shortcuts

Readers' tips to make your beading life easier

1 clip it
When working on a wire or stringing project, a pair of nail clippers is handy for making quick, close cuts. Clippers also relieve hand strain; you can trim with one hand, rather than hold a set of wire cutters with one hand and pull the wire taut with the other.
– JULIA PRATER, VIA E-MAIL

2 squeaky clean
Sterling or gold-filled wire is often sold in coils, taped together. To remove tape residue, use an adhesive remover such as Goo Gone. Simply moisten a rag and rub it on the wire for low-effort cleaning.
– VERONICA STEWART, VIA E-MAIL

3 swap meet
My friends and I get together not only to make jewelry, but to swap beads and ideas. Spending time with one another helps stir our creative juices and encourages new possibilities for old beads. Plus, one person's trash truly can be another person's treasure.
– T. DUNCAN, VIA E-MAIL

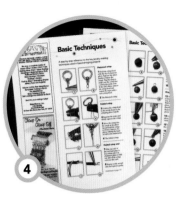

4 convenient reference
I removed the Basic Techniques section of *BeadStyle* and laminated each page at a copy store. I put the sheets on my bulletin board or in my bead box for easy reference. That way, there's no need to flip pages back and forth as I work on a project in the magazine.
– B. EARL, DENVER, CO

5 board again
Dust, broken beads, and tiny pieces of wire often get stuck in the channels of a bead design board. To clean the board, use a piece of mailing or packing tape. Just push the tape into the channels and corners to remove the dust. Your board will look brand new!
– CHERYL CASSIDY, SPRINGFIELD, MA

Mixed

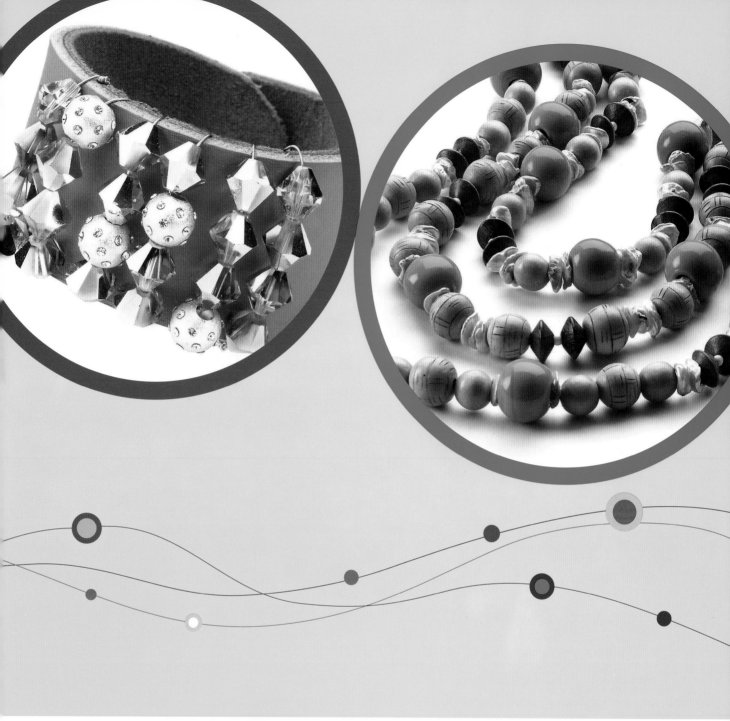

media

Make a
memory-wire
choker without
a clasp

by Jane Shafrin

Wonderful
memory

The trick to this wrap choker is the resilience of memory wire. Thread small beads on one coil to form the foundation. Link dangles with fabulous focal and accent beads to bring all the attention to the front.

Supply List

- 16-in. (41cm) strand 3-5mm beads
- **2** 24mm focal beads and a 17-21mm focal bead (Randy Smith's art beads from Eclectica, 262-641-0910, eclecticabeads.com)
- 13mm accent bead
- 7-8mm accent bead
- **6** bead caps to fit focal beads
- assorted spacers (**12–14** 2-3mm, **4** 5mm, **1–3** 3mm, and **3–5** 3mm round)
- memory wire, necklace diameter

- 12 in. (30cm) 22-gauge wire or **3** 3-in. (7.6cm) eye pins and a 1½-in. (3.8cm) eye pin
- 1½-in. head pin
- 3-in. head pin
- chainnose and roundnose pliers
- diagonal wire cutters
- heavy-duty wire cutters (optional)

1. Wrap a coil of memory wire around your neck so it fits comfortably. (The black necklace is 13 in./33cm; the green, 15 in./38cm.) Add 1 in. (2.5cm) and cut the wire to that length. Cut with heavy-duty wire cutters or grab the wire with chainnose pliers and bend it back and forth at one place until it breaks. Memory wire will damage diagonal wire cutters.

Make a loop at one end. String 3-5mm beads on the wire until the beads are within ½ in. (1.3cm) of the end. Make a loop at the end.

> **EDITOR'S TIP**
> Memory wire is both stiff and brittle. To make a loop at the end, roll the loop rather than trying to make a perfect lollipop-shaped plain loop.

Contact Jane at (800) 572-7920, janey@beadsbymail.com, or visit beadsbymail.com.

2. Form the long dangle's units. First, string two or three spacer beads and the 13mm accent bead on a 1½-in. (3.8cm) head pin.

Second, cut two 3-in. (7.6cm) pieces of 22-gauge wire and make a plain loop (Basic Techniques, p. 12) at one end of each, or use an eye pin. On one eye pin, string four spacers, a bead cap, 24mm focal bead, bead cap, and spacer.

Third, cut a 1½-in. piece of wire and make a plain loop at one end, or use an eye pin. String the 7-8mm accent bead.

Fourth, on the remaining 3-in. eye pin, string one or two spacers, a bead cap, the 17-21mm focal bead, a bead cap, and one or two spacers.

Make a plain loop above the top bead in each unit.

3. To assemble the long dangle, link the 13mm bead unit to the bottom of the 24mm bead unit by opening and closing the loops. Working from left to right as illustrated in photo B, link each unit to the bottom of the next.

4. Form the short dangle's units. First, string four spacers, a bead cap, 24mm focal bead, bead cap, and three spacers on a 3-in. head pin.

Second, cut a 3-in. piece of wire and make a plain loop at one end, or use an eye pin. String three spacers, a 3-5mm bead, spacer, 3-5mm bead, spacer, and 3-5mm bead.

Make a plain loop above the top bead in each unit.

5. To assemble the short dangle, link the head pin unit to the eye pin unit.

6. Open the loop at the top of a dangle, string one loop of the choker, and close the loop. Repeat on the other end of the choker with the remaining dangle. ❖

The
charm

by Gita Marie Sturm

Embellish vibrant enameled charms with beads for whimsical earrings or a playful pendant

Brilliant sterling silver shines through these delicate enameled charms to give each a soft watercolor quality. The glass enamel coating, however, ensures strength and durability. Enhance your pieces with lustrous pearls, crystals, and gemstones you have on hand.

A

earrings • 1. String two head pins with a bicone, two chips, and a bicone. String one head pin with a bicone, two chips, a round crystal, a bead cap, and a bicone. Make a plain loop (Basic Techniques, p. 12) above the top bead on each head pin.

B

2. Open the loop on the longer head pin and attach it to the enamel finding's center loop. Close the loop. Attach the remaining head pins to the remaining loops.

C

3. Open the loop on an earring wire and attach the enamel finding. Close the loop. Make a second earring to match the first.

pendant • 1. Follow steps 1 and 2 of the earrings or create a design of your own.

2. Open the loop on the bail (Basic Techniques) and attach the enamel finding. Make sure the decorative side of each component is facing forward. Close the loop.

Slide the pendant's bail on a pre-finished organza necklace. ✤

SupplyList

earrings
- **2** three-loop enamel findings (Gita Maria, 541-247-9647, gitamaria.com)
- **12** 4-6mm gemstone chips
- **12** 4mm bicone crystals, **6** each of 2 colors
- **2** 6mm round crystals
- **2** 7mm bead caps
- **6** 1½-in. (3.8cm) decorative head pins
- pair of earring wires
- chainnose and roundnose pliers
- diagonal wire cutters

pendant
- three-loop enamel finding (Gita Maria)
- **6** 4-6mm gemstone chips
- **6** 4mm bicone crystals, **3** each of 2 colors
- 6mm round crystal
- 7mm bead cap
- **3** 1½-in. decorative head pins
- pendant bail (Gita Maria)
- pre-finished organza ribbon necklace
- chainnose and roundnose pliers
- diagonal wire cutters

Contact Gita at PO Box 918, Gold Beach, OR 97444, (541) 247-9647, or visit gitamaria.com.

of enamel

Bejeweled cuff

by Linda Osterhoudt

Wire a group of distinctive beads to a leather cuff

Once you try your hand at these simple bracelets, you'll be hooked. Thirty minutes and some basic wire wrapping will produce a stylish, eye-catching piece of jewelry. Whether you prefer a turquoise chunk, '80s punk, or bohemian funk, you're bound to make several of these clever cuffs.

SupplyList

- **15-30** assorted shapes and sizes of gemstones, crystals, and spacers
- 1¼-in. (3.2cm) wide leather cuff bracelet (Linda O...Oh Linda, ohlinda.com for stores)
- 24- or 26-gauge wire
- chainnose pliers
- diagonal wire cutters

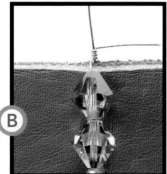

1. On your work surface, arrange your beads in columns 1¼-in. (3.2cm) long. Center the cuff above the arrangement. Make a dot on the back to show where to start attaching the beads.

Cut a 24-in. (61cm) piece of wire. String the first column of beads 3 in. (7.6cm) from the wire's end. Bend the longer part of the wire around the back of the cuff at the dot.

2. Wrap the shorter wire around the longer one, as in a wrapped loop (Basic Techniques, p. 12). Trim the excess wrapping wire.

3. Wrap the remaining wire snugly around the back of the cuff.

String the next column of beads and wrap the wire around the cuff. Repeat until you have attached each column of beads to the cuff.

4. Pass the wire under the last wrap on the upper edge of the cuff three or four times and trim the excess wire. ❖

Contact Linda at lindaoohlinda@earthlink.net, (561) 202-7575, or visit ohlinda.com.

The tropics beckon with an eclectic mix of wood, bone, shell, and ocean blue ceramic beads. Create different bead mixes for the inner two strands; pool them together to form the longest. This necklace is such a breeze to string, you'll be able to accessorize your sundress, slip into your sandals, and coast through the summer in style.

Isle be

A bounty of nature's beads blends with ease in a three-strand necklace

1. Determine the finished length of your necklace. (These strands are 17½, 18½, and 19½ in./44.5, 47, and 49.5cm, respectively.) Add 6 in. (15cm) to each measurement and cut a piece of beading wire to each length. Center a 16mm round on the shortest wire.

2. On each end, string two chips, a 10mm, two chips, a rondelle, a 3mm, a rondelle, two chips, a 10mm, two chips, and a 16mm. Repeat this pattern until the strand is within 1 in. (2.5cm) of the desired length. Tape each end.

stylin'

by Paulette Biedenbender

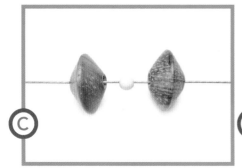

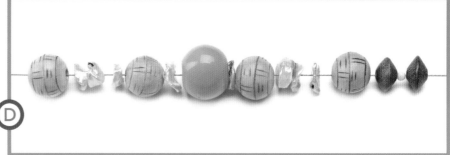

3. Center a rondelle, 3mm round, and rondelle on the middle wire.

4. On each end, string a 12mm, three chips, 12mm, chip, 16mm, chip, 12mm, three chips, 12mm, rondelle, 3mm, and a rondelle. Repeat this pattern until the strand is within 1 in. of the desired length. Tape each end.

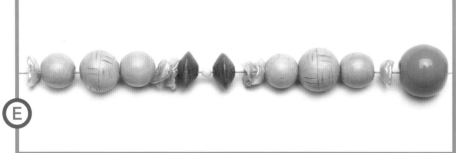

5. On the longest wire, center a 16mm round as in step 1.

6. On each end, string a chip, 10mm, 12mm, 10mm, two chips, rondelle, 3mm, rondelle, two chips, 10mm, 12mm, 10mm, a chip, and a 16mm. Repeat this pattern until the strand is within 1 in. of the desired length. Tape each end.

7. Remove the tape from one end of each strand. String three 3mm rounds, a crimp bead, a 3mm, and the respective loop on half the clasp. Go back through the last beads strung and tighten the wires. Repeat on the other end. Check the fit, and add or remove an equal number of beads from each end, if necessary. Crimp the crimp beads (Basic Techniques, p. 12) and trim the excess wire. ❖

SupplyList

- 12-in. (30cm) strand 16mm round ceramic beads (ceramic and wooden beads available from Planet Bead, 800-889-4365)
- 16-in. (41cm) strand 12mm round wooden beads
- 16-in. strand 11mm wooden rondelles
- 16-in. strand 10mm round wooden beads
- 16-in. strand 3mm round cow bone beads (Fire Mountain Gems, 800-355-2137, firemountaingems.com)
- 16-in. strand 6-10mm shell chips
- flexible beading wire, .014 or .015
- **6** crimp beads
- three-strand bar clasp (Jade Mountain Bead Co., 608-256-5233)
- chainnose or crimping pliers
- diagonal wire cutters

EDITOR'S TIP

Want to create your own pattern or alter the necklace's length? Before stringing, arrange the largest beads on a design board. Then fill in the spaces with your own pattern. This will ensure uniform spacing among the strands.

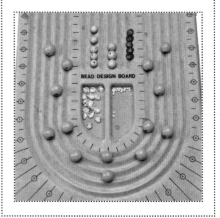

Contact Paulette in care of BeadStyle.

Linear

1. Determine the finished length of your earrings. (The gold earrings' strands are 4 and 5 in./10 and 13cm; the silver strands, 2½ and 3 in./6.4 and 7.6cm.) Add the lengths together, add 5 in., and cut a piece of beading wire to that length. Fold the wire, leaving one end 1 in. (2.5cm) longer than the other. String a crimp bead over both ends, leaving a small loop between the bead and the fold. Flatten the crimp bead (Basic Techniques, p. 12).

2. On each strand, string tube-shaped beads, adding accent beads when the strand is within ½ in. (1.3cm) of the desired length. String a tube, crimp bead, and seed bead. Skipping the seed bead, go back through the beads just strung. Tighten the wires and flatten the crimp beads.

SupplyList

- 2-4g 3-4mm tube-shaped beads (gold-filled or liquid silver, Rio Grande, 800-545-6566)
- accent beads or crystals
- **4** size 11º Japanese cylinder beads
- flexible beading wire, .010 or .012
- **6** 1mm crimp beads
- pair of post earrings with loop
- chainnose pliers
- diagonal wire cutters

3. Open the loop on an earring post and attach the dangle's loop. Make a second earring the mirror image of the first. ✤

Contact Cynthia at cynnyc1@rogers.com.

These long and linear earrings are perfect for the girl who blazes her own trail. Sleek, slender lines take you effortlessly from day to night, season to season. Two columns of tube beads sway below simple posts. For high drama, string 5-inch dangles.

thinking

by Cynthia Williams

String daringly long earrings with tubes and accent beads

The ring's

the thing

String a multitude of crystal and silver rings

by Carolyn Sheahan

Elegant but not understated, these dazzling rings catch every errant ray of light. Two simple stringing techniques produce an array of styles, depending on your choice of beads. Go for maximum zing with rhinestone rondelles, or tone down the look with subtle silver. Once you start stringing, one sparkling ring will lead quickly to another.

silver ring • 1. Determine the finished length of your ring, add 3 in. (7.6cm), and cut a piece of beading wire to that length. Center 3mm and 4mm beads on the wire, and string seed beads on each side until the ring is the desired length.

2. String a crimp bead on one wire, and pass the other wire through in the opposite direction. Go through an additional seed bead on each side. Pull the wires tight and check the fit. Add or remove seed beads, if necessary.

3. Make a folded crimp (Basic Techniques, p. 12) and trim the excess wire.

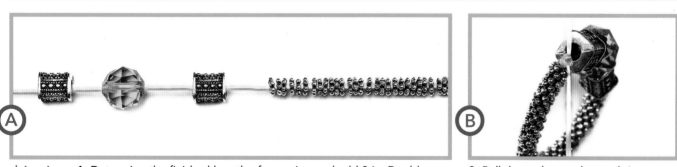

daisy ring • 1. Determine the finished length of your ring and add 3 in. Double that measurement, and cut a piece of elastic to that length. Center a twisted-wire beading needle on the elastic and tape the ends together.

2. String an accent bead, a crystal, and an accent bead. String spacers until the ring is the desired length. Check the fit, and add or remove spacers, if necessary.

3. Pull the ends together and tie a surgeon's knot (Basic Techniques). Glue the knot and trim the ends. Gently pull the ring to slide the knot into the accent bead's hole.

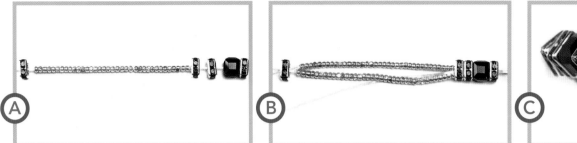

A

B

C

double-strand cube ring • 1. Determine the finished length of your ring and add 3 in. Cut two pieces of elastic to that length. Thread a twisted-wire beading needle on one strand of elastic.

2. String a squaredelle and approximately 1½ in. (3.8cm) of seed beads on the elastic. String two squaredelles, a cube, and a squaredelle. Remove the needle.

3. Thread the needle on the second piece of elastic and pass it through the first squaredelle. String a length of seed beads equal to the first strand. Pass the needle through the squaredelles, cube, and squaredelle.

4. Check the fit, and add or remove seed beads from each strand, if necessary. Pull the ends together and tie a surgeon's knot. Glue the knot and trim the ends. Hide the knot between the two squaredelles.

A

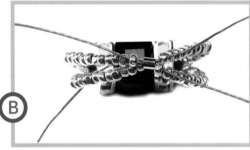

B

C

dazzling double-strand ring • 1. Determine the finished length of your ring, add 3 in., and cut two pieces of beading wire to that length. Center a bicone, squaredelle, cube, squaredelle, and bicone over both wires. Separate the wires, and string seed beads on each end of each wire until the ring is the desired length.

2. String a crimp bead over both wires on one end, and pass the other ends through the crimp bead in the opposite direction. Go through an additional seed bead on each strand. Pull the wires tight and check the fit. Add or remove seed beads, if necessary.

3. Make a folded crimp and trim the excess wire. ✤

STANDARD RING SIZES

SIZE 5	2 in.	5.1cm
SIZE 6	2⅛ in.	5.4cm
SIZE 7	2¼ in.	5.7cm
SIZE 8	2⅜ in.	6.0 cm

Contact Carolyn in care of BeadStyle.

SupplyList

silver ring
- 4mm cube, Hill Tribes silver
- **2** 3mm cubes, Hill Tribes silver
- **4** 3mm discs, silver
- 1g size 11º faceted seed beads, silver
- crimp bead
- flexible beading wire, .014 or .015
- crimping pliers
- diagonal wire cutters

daisy ring
- 6-8mm round crystal
- **2** 5 x 6mm large-hole accent beads
- **60-70** 2mm flat spacers
- ribbon elastic
- twisted-wire beading needle, medium
- G-S Hypo Cement
- scissors

double-strand cube ring
- 6mm cube-shaped crystal
- **4** 6mm squaredelles
- 1g size 11º faceted seed beads, silver
- ribbon elastic
- twisted-wire beading needle, medium
- G-S Hypo Cement
- scissors

dazzling double-strand ring
- 8mm cube-shaped crystal
- **2** 8mm squaredelles
- **2** 4mm bicone crystals
- 1g size 11º faceted seed beads, silver
- crimp bead
- flexible beading wire, .014 or .015
- crimping pliers
- diagonal wire cutters

Charming twist

A custom pendant adds punch to a cord bracelet

by Jane Konkel

Add your favorite focal bead and a gemstone box clasp to a length of upholstery cord for a contemporary take on a traditional charm bracelet. Or, simplify the process by purchasing a cord bracelet with a clasp already attached. For versatility, make several charms and attach a small lobster clasp, so you can change charms whenever you like.

1. String a pearl, bead cap, focal bead, and spacer on a decorative head pin. Make the first half of a wrapped loop (Basic Techniques, p. 12) above the spacer.

2. Attach the loop to the bail and complete the wraps.

3. Determine the finished length of your bracelet. Subtract the length of the clasp and cut a piece of twisted cord to that length, taping before you cut. Make sure that ⅛ in. (3mm) of tape remains on each end. Trim the excess tape. Apply Fray Check or nail polish to the exposed cord ends. Allow to dry.

4. Center the pendant on the cord.

5. Apply glue to the inside of a crimp end. Place one end of the cord into the crimp end, covering the tape. Fold down the sides of the crimp end (Basic Techniques). Allow to dry. Repeat on the other end.

6. Open a jump ring (Basic Techniques) and attach a crimp end and half the clasp. Close the jump ring. Repeat on the other end with the remaining clasp half. ❖

223

Rainbow

Multicolored tourmaline and crystals unite
with gold in a necklace, bracelet, and earring set

Clashing hues of tourmaline look harmonious when paired with brilliant
crystals in a spectrum of colors. Buy a mixed bag of round crystals and avoid
stringing a red-to-violet continuum of beads. Instead, group gemstone colors
together and punctuate with crystals in a more saturated tone. Add some wee pots
of gold – a butterfly and a few spacers – and these pieces will brighten any rainy day.

(A)

(B)

necklace • 1. String a crystal on a head pin and make the first
half of a wrapped loop (Basic Techniques, p. 12). Attach this
loop to the loop on a butterfly charm. Complete the wraps.

2. Determine the finished length of your necklace. (The
shortest strand in this necklace is 14¼ in./36cm.) Add 6 in.
(15cm) and cut a piece of beading wire to that length. Cut two
more pieces, each 1 in. (2.5cm) longer than the first strand.

3. On the shortest wire, string 5 in. (13cm) of tourmaline,
interspersed with crystals and 3mm spacers as desired. Create
a multicolored effect by alternating groups of pink, brown,
and green stones with matching crystals.

String 5¼ in. (13.3cm) of beads and spacers on one of the
remaining wires, arranging the beads so that the two strands
contain different colors.

by Naomi Fujimoto

connection

4. Center the butterfly on the remaining wire. Alternating shades of tourmaline and crystals, string assorted beads and spacers on each side until the length is 5¼ in. Check the drape of the necklace and string additional beads on the wires, if necessary.

5. On each end, string a spacer bar onto the respective wires. String approximately 2 in. (5cm) of beads. Repeat one or more times until the necklace is the desired length, allowing 2 in. for finishing.

6. On each end, string a spacer bar, 3mm spacer, crystal, crimp bead, crystal, and spacer. Pass each wire through a loop of a three-strand clasp; make sure to position each clasp half correctly. Go back through the last beads strung, tighten the wires, and crimp the crimp beads (Basic Techniques). (The strands will hang more evenly if you finish the middle strand first.) Trim the excess wire.

bracelet • Determine the finished length of your bracelet, add 5 in., and cut three pieces of beading wire to that length.

String 2 in. of tourmaline, crystals, and 3mm spacers on each wire. (Refer to step 3 of the necklace for color placement suggestions.) String a spacer bar onto the respective wires. Repeat two or more times until the bracelet is the desired length, allowing 2 in. for finishing. Do not string a spacer bar after your last beaded section. Follow step 6 of the necklace to finish the ends of the bracelet, omitting the 3mm spacers.

earrings • **1.** String a 6mm crystal and a spacer onto a head pin. Make the first half of a wrapped loop above the spacer.

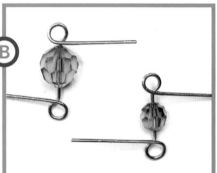

2. Snip the heads off two head pins. String a 6mm crystal on one wire and a 4mm on the other. Make the first half of a wrapped loop ⅛ in. (3mm) from the bead on each end.

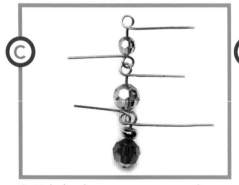

3. Link the three components as shown and complete the wraps.

4. Open the loop on an earring wire. Attach the top loop of the dangle to the earring wire and close the loop. Make a second earring to match the first. ✣

Supply List

necklace
- 3 16-in. (.41m) strands 6 x 7mm oval tourmaline
- butterfly charm, approx. 10 x 16mm
- **60-70** 6mm round crystals, assorted colors
- **30-40** 3mm flat spacers
- **6-10** three-strand spacer bars
- 1½-in. (38mm) head pin
- flexible beading wire, .014 or .015
- **6** crimp beads
- three-strand slide clasp
- chainnose and roundnose pliers
- diagonal wire cutters
- crimping pliers (optional)

bracelet
- 16-in. strand 6 x 7mm oval tourmaline
- **30-40** 6mm round crystals, assorted colors
- **10-20** 3mm flat spacers
- **4 or 5** three-strand spacer bars
- flexible beading wire, .014 or .015
- **6** crimp beads
- three-strand slide clasp
- chainnose or crimping pliers
- diagonal wire cutters

earrings
- **4** 6mm round crystals, **2** each of 2 colors
- **2** 4mm round crystals
- **2** 3mm flat spacers
- **6** 2-in. (51mm) head pins
- pair of earring wires
- chainnose and roundnose pliers
- diagonal wire cutters

HOOP
dreams

Embellish hoop earrings with gemstones and pearls

by Jill Italiano

You've seen the chandeliers – now it's time to add some hoops to round out the season's earring collection. This pair boasts tiny gemstones in a funky fringe. One technique – the handy plain loop – is all you'll need. Don't forget to keep both your gemstones and your attitude light.

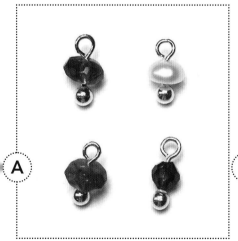

(A)

(B)

SupplyList

- **28** or more 3-4mm gemstones or pearls, such as rondelles, faceted round beads, and button-shaped pearls
- pair of hoop earrings with hanging loops, approx. 27mm (Rio Grande, 800-545-6566)
- **28** or more 1-in. (25mm) decorative head pins
- chainnose and roundnose pliers
- diagonal wire cutters

1. String each rondelle, faceted round bead, and pearl on a head pin. Make a plain loop (Basic Techniques, p. 12) above each bead.

2. Open a loop on a dangle (Basic Techniques), attach it to an earring loop, and close the loop. Attach a second dangle to the same loop. Continue to attach pairs of dangles to each earring loop. Make a second earring to match the first. ❖

Contact Jill at jill@bellaoro.com or view her collection at jillidesigns.com.

Pattern play

by Anne Nikolai Kloss

Carved beads in muted colors create an earthy multistrand necklace

Creating and manipulating patterns is a rudimentary part of our elementary math and art classes. As adults, we transform that basic knowledge into pieces of art – especially wearable art. Color patterns are the foundation of most beaded jewelry; experiment with simple to complex pattern variations. Before stringing, lay out the carved beads to get placement ideas – for example, separate light and dark tones or keep them mixed. Stagger the varied carved bead lengths and alternate the two seed bead colors between the carved beads and from strand to strand to create subtle pattern and color transitioning.

SupplyList

- **40** assorted carved horn and bone beads, 20-38mm (Planet Bead, 800-889-4365)
- 20g size 6º seed beads, matte black
- 20g size 6º seed beads, gold
- **50** 4mm brass nuggets or 5g size 6º seed beads, metallic bronze
- 16-in. (.41m) strand 3mm triangular brass spacers (Planet Bead)
- **10** 3mm spacer beads
- **10** crimp beads
- five-strand clasp (Ashes to Beauty, 505-899-8864)
- flexible beading wire, .014 or .015
- chainnose or crimping pliers
- diagonal wire cutters

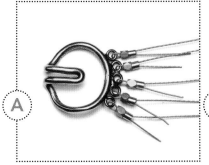

1. Determine the finished length of your necklace. (This one is 24 in./61cm.) Add 6 in. (15cm) and cut five strands of beading wire to that length.

String a crimp bead, a 3mm bead, and a clasp loop on each strand. Go back through these beads and crimp the crimp beads (Basic Techniques, p. 12).

2. String a varied amount of size 6º seed beads on each strand, covering the wire tails and alternating the colors on the strands.

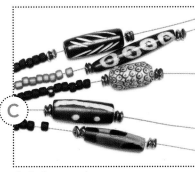

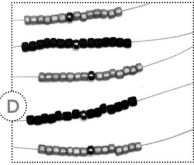

3. String two brass spacers, a carved bead, and two brass spacers on each strand.

4. String seven size 6ºs, a bronze seed bead or 4mm brass nugget, and seven size 6ºs.

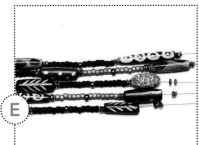

5. Repeat steps 3 and 4 until you have strung seven or eight carved beads on each strand, depending on your desired length. End with a carved bead pattern on each strand.

Contact Anne at annekloss@mac.com.

6. String size 6º seed beads until each strand is within 1 in. (2.5cm) of the desired length. String a crimp bead, a 3mm bead, and the respective loop on the remaining clasp half. Go back through the beads just strung plus one or two more. Tighten the wires, check the fit, and add or remove an equal number of beads on each strand, if necessary. Crimp the crimp beads and trim the excess wires. ❖

Living large

Look like a leading lady in a powerfully feminine necklace

by Gail Lannum

You are strong, confident, and able to see the big picture. The requisite for such a woman of substance: substantial accoutrements. Resin and glass beads accompanied by a huge silver pendant loom large, but not heavy. One tempting aspect about working with these Amazonian beads is that only a few are necessary for a prominent piece. So, go ahead – live large.

Supply List

necklace

- large silver pendant, approx. 40-55mm (The Bead Goes On, 866-861-2323, beadgoeson.com)
- **2** 14 x 20mm silver accent beads
- **10** 14-18mm glass or resin beads (green glass from The Bead Goes On, pink dice resin from Natural Touch Beads, 707-781-0808, naturaltouchbeads.com)
- 16-in. (41cm) strand 6-8mm glass or resin beads (The Bead Goes On)
- **12** 6-8mm flat spacers
- flexible beading wire, .024
- **2** crimp beads
- silver toggle clasp (clasp on pink necklace from Saki Silver, 513-861-9626, sakisilver.com)
- chainnose or crimping pliers
- diagonal wire cutters

earrings

- **2** 14 x 20mm silver accent beads
- **4** 6-8mm glass or resin beads, left over from necklace
- **4** or **8** 4mm flat spacer beads
- **2** 2½-in. (6.4cm) plain or decorative head pins
- pair of earring wires
- chainnose and roundnose pliers
- diagonal wire cutters

Contact Gail at (440) 899-0649 or moonriverbeads@aol.com.

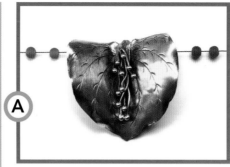

necklace • 1. Determine the finished length of your necklace. (The green necklace is 16 in./41cm; the pink, 18 in./46cm.) Add 6 in. (15cm) and cut a piece of beading wire to that length. Center the pendant on the wire and string 6-8mm beads on each side until they extend beyond the edges of the pendant.

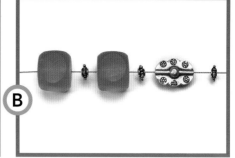

2. On each end, string a 14-18mm dice bead, spacer, 14-18mm bead, spacer, accent, and a spacer.

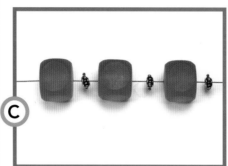

3. On each end, string an alternating pattern of three 14-18mm beads and three spacers. String 6-8mm beads on each end until the strand is within 1 in. (2.5cm) of the desired length.

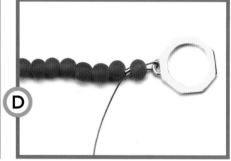

4. On each end, string a crimp bead, 6-8mm bead, and half the clasp. Go back through the beads just strung and tighten the wire. Check the fit, and add or remove beads from each end, if necessary. Crimp the crimp beads (Basic Techniques p. 12) and trim the excess wire.

earrings • 1. String a spacer (optional) 6-8mm bead, spacer, accent, spacer, 6-8mm bead, and a spacer (optional) on a head pin. Make a wrapped loop (Basic Techniques) above the top bead.

2. Open the loop on an earring wire and attach the dangle. Close the loop. Make a second earring to match the first. ❖

Dramatic
pairing

by Erica Dean

Diverse elements
converge in a richly
textured necklace
and earring set

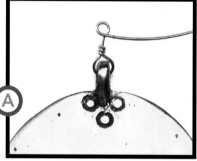

Although the centerpiece of this necklace is a bold metal pendant, red coral or golden amber chips and matching seed beads add an intense punch of color. The shapely chips also contrast with the pendant's smoothness, providing an intriguing interplay of textures. Make a necklace with rich colors to complement jewel-tone wardrobe pieces, adding a pair of simple yet distinctive earrings for the finishing touch.

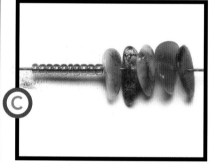

necklace • 1. Cut a 3½-in. (9cm) piece of 22-gauge wire. Using the largest part of your roundnose pliers, make the first half of a wrapped loop 2 in. (5cm) from one end of the wire (Basic Techniques, p. 12). Attach the loop to the pendant's bail and complete the wraps.

2. Make the first half of a wrapped loop ⅛ in. (3mm) above the completed wraps.

3. Attach the pendant's loop to the tube bead's loop and complete the wraps.

4. Determine the finished length of your necklace. (The shorter strands in these necklaces are 15½ in./ 39cm.; the longer strands, 16½ in./ 42cm.) Add 6 in. (15cm) to each measurement and cut a piece of beading wire to those lengths. On the longer strand, center the tube bead with three chips on each side.

5. On each end, string 10 or more seed beads and ½ in. (1.3cm) of chips. Repeat until the strand is within 1 in. (2.5cm) of the desired length, ending with seed beads.

6. On the shorter strand, center ½ in. of chips. Then, string 12 or more seed beads and ½ in. of chips on each end. Repeat until the strand is within 1 in. of the desired length, ending with seed beads.

7. On one end of both strands, string a crimp bead, a seed bead, and the respective loop of half the clasp. Go back through the beads plus a few more and tighten each wire. Repeat on the other end. Check the fit and add or remove beads from each end, if necessary. Crimp the crimp beads (Basic Techniques) and trim the excess wire.

Supply List

all projects
- chainnose and roundnose pliers
- diagonal wire cutters

coral necklace
- 52mm round metal pendant (Planet Bead, 800-889-4365)
- 16-in. (41cm) strand 4-7mm coral chips
- hank size 10º or 11º seed beads, red
- 29mm tube bead with loop (Fire Mountain Gems, 800-355-2137, firemountaingems.com)
- flexible beading wire, .014 or .015
- 3½ in. (9cm) 22-gauge wire
- **4** crimp beads
- two-strand clasp
- crimping pliers (optional)

amber necklace
- 52mm round metal pendant
- 16-in. strand 4-7mm amber chips
- hank size 10º or 11º seed beads, amber-colored
- 22mm tube bead with loop (Eclectica, 262-641-0910, eclecticabeads.com)
- flexible beading wire, .014 or .015
- 3½ in. 22-gauge wire
- **4** crimp beads
- two-strand clasp
- crimping pliers (optional)

earrings
- **2** 15mm disc-shaped beads
- leftover seed beads
- **2** 1½-in. (3.8cm) decorative head pins
- pair of decorative earring wires
- **2** 4mm flat spacers (optional)

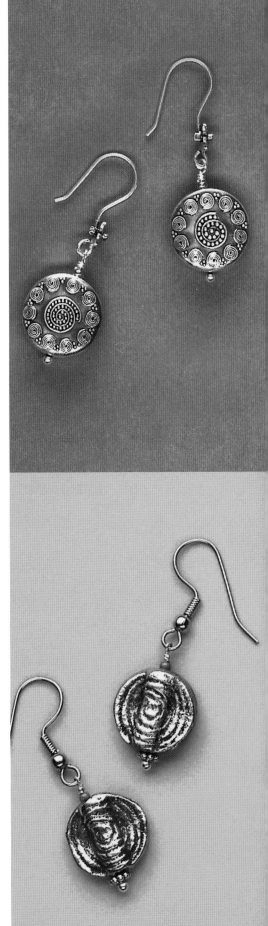

earrings • 1. String a spacer (if desired), a disc bead, and a seed bead on a 1½-in. (3.8cm) head pin. Make a wrapped loop (Basic Techniques) above the seed bead.

2. Open the loop on an earring wire and attach the dangle. Close the loop. Make a second earring to match the first. ❖

Contact Erica at (240) 463-2969 or edean879@yahoo.com.

Try tribal

Beads of natural materials adorn a double-strand necklace

by Ronna Sarvas Weltman

Tribal influences are sprouting up everywhere. To keep the look primitive, select African trade beads, Hill Tribes silver, and beads of bone, horn, shell, and wood. String a single strand for a more masculine look, or go native and string this two-strand necklace for the earth mother in you.

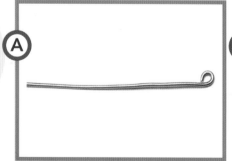

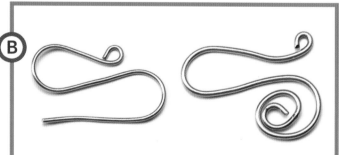

clasp • **1.** Cut a 5-in. (13cm) piece of 16-gauge wire. With roundnose pliers, make a loop at one end of the wire.

2. Using your fingers and chainnose pliers, curve the wire into an S shape.

3. Position the roundnose pliers at the straight end of the wire. Coil the wire to form a spiral.

4. Hammer both sides of the clasp.

necklace • 1. Determine the finished length of your necklace. (The longer strand measures 15 in./38cm; the shorter strand is 13½ in./34cm.) Add 6 in. (15cm) to each measurement and cut a piece of beading wire to each length.

2. On the longer strand, center two bone disc beads, a heishi, bead cap, focal bead, bead cap, heishi, and two bone discs.

3. On each end, string a pattern similar to the one shown or create one of your own.

4. Continue stringing trade beads until the strand is within 2 in. (5cm) of the desired length. Tape the ends.

5. On the shorter strand, center a heishi, round bone, silver oval, round bone, and a heishi.

6. On each end, string a pattern similar to the one shown or create one of your own.

7. Continue stringing trade beads until the strand is within 2 in. of the desired length.

8. Remove the tape from the longer strand. String a crimp bead and a trade bead on each end. String one end of each strand through a jump ring. Go back through the beads just strung. Repeat on the other end.

9. Tighten the wires, check the fit, and add or remove beads if necessary. Crimp the crimp beads (Basic Techniques, p. 12) and trim the excess wire. Attach the clasp to one of the jump rings. ❧

Contact Ronna at ronnaround@comcast.net.

Supply List

- barrel-shaped bone or wood focal bead, 18 x 22mm or 16 x 28mm (all beads available at Planet Bead, 800-889-4365)
- 24 x 4mm oval silver bead
- **4** 14mm disc-shaped bone beads
- **2** 22mm or **4** 14mm silver accent beads
- 16-in. (41cm) strand African trade beads
- 16-in. strand 4-5mm brown and black heishi beads
- **2** 10mm silver bead caps
- **18-22** 4-6mm silver spacers, rounds, and barrels
- **6** 5 x 12mm silver tube beads
- **4** 5 x 6mm wood black crow beads
- **16-20** 4-8mm round and tube-shaped bone beads
- flexible beading wire, .014 or .015
- 5 in. (13cm) 16-gauge wire, half hard
- **4** crimp beads
- **2** 10mm soldered jump rings
- chainnose and roundnose pliers
- diagonal wire cutters
- crimping pliers (optional)
- ball-peen hammer
- bench block or anvil

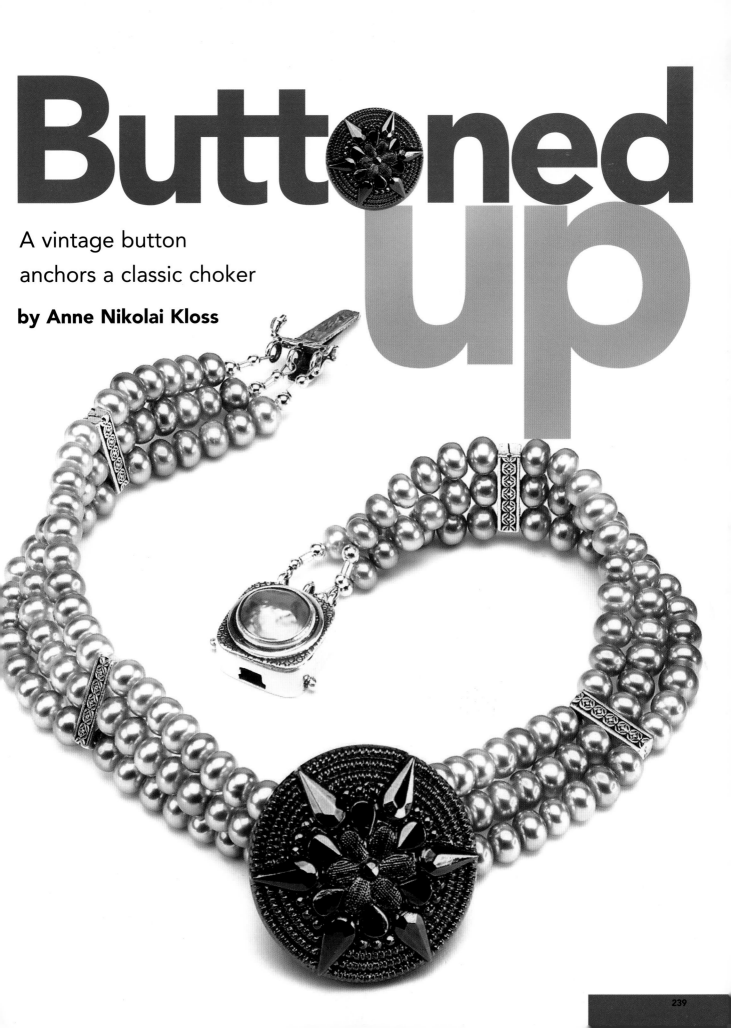

Buttoned up

A vintage button
anchors a classic choker

by Anne Nikolai Kloss

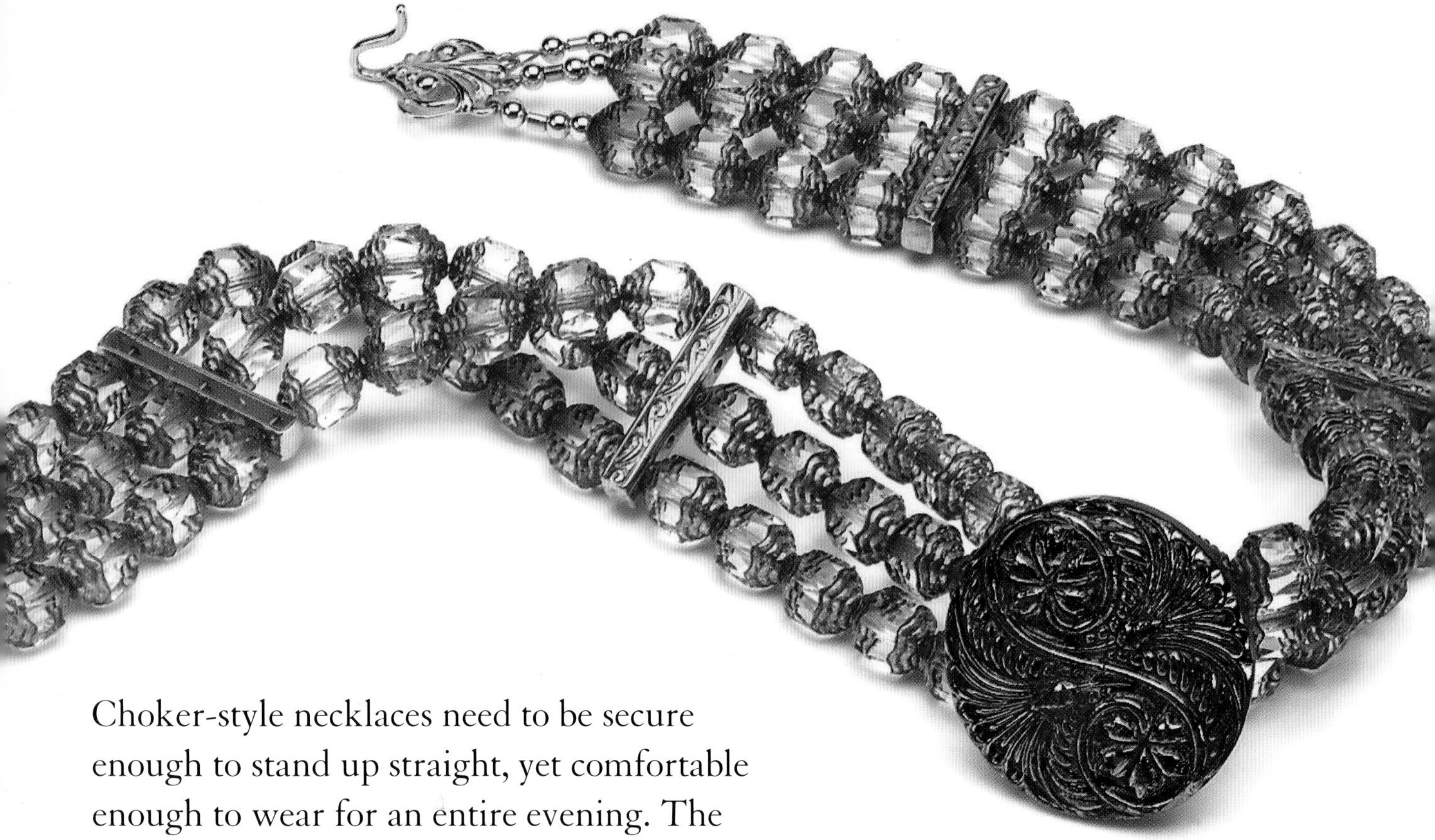

Choker-style necklaces need to be secure enough to stand up straight, yet comfortable enough to wear for an entire evening. The key to a great fit is the bead count: The drape is controlled by changing the number of beads in the middle section, with the snugness determined at the end. For this project, start searching through your button box — or purchase a new or vintage button. Then, accent the button with elegant pearls or translucent Czech glass, depending on your personal style. The resulting one-of-a-kind choker will be a perfect blend of comfort and beauty.

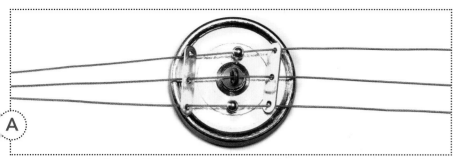

1. Determine the finished length of your choker. (This one is 15 in./38cm.) Add 6 in. (15cm) and cut three strands of wire to that length.

2. String a plain spacer bar over all three wires. String a 3mm bead on the top wire, the button shank on the middle wire, and a 3mm bead on the bottom wire. String another spacer bar over all three wires. (The 3mm beads should equal the width of the shank. If not, use a smaller or larger diameter bead to fill the space.) Center the button, beads, and spacer bars over all three wires, as shown.

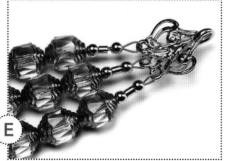

3. On each end, string 2 in. (5cm) of accent beads. Count the number of beads.

4. String a decorative spacer bar on each end.

5. On each end of the top wire, string one fewer than the number of accent beads in step 3. On the middle row, string the same number of accent beads as in step 3. On the bottom wire, string one more than the number of accent beads in step 3. String a decorative spacer bar on each end.

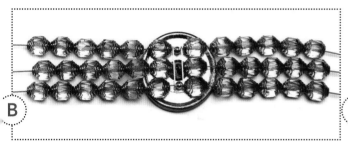

6. String 1½ in. (3.8cm) of accent beads on each end of each wire. Check the fit, allowing for the length of the clasp. Add or remove an equal number of beads from each side, if necessary.

7. On each wire, string a 3mm spacer bead, crimp bead, 3mm spacer, and a clasp half. Go back through the beads just strung and a few more. Repeat on the other side. Tighten the wires and check the fit again. Add or remove beads, if necessary. (If you need to adjust the fit by a size smaller than the length of one of your accent beads, add or remove spacer beads on each end, but keep one spacer between the crimp and the clasp for security.) Crimp the crimp beads (Basic Techniques, p. 12), beginning with the center strand. Trim the excess wire. ❖

Supply List

• 35-45mm flat-backed (not concave) button (The Button Shoppe, 888-254-6078 buttonshoppe.com)
• **100-150** 4-8mm accent beads (the total length of the beads should equal three times your basic necklace length)
• **4** 3- or 5-hole decorative spacer bars, with a length equal to three accent beads
• **2** 3-hole plain spacer bars
• **16** or more 3mm round beads
• flexible beading wire, .014 or .015
• **6** crimp beads
• **3**-strand clasp
• chainnose or crimping pliers
• diagonal wire cutters

Contact Anne at annekloss@mac.com.

Definitely
demure

Pastel hues
blend
beautifully
in a faceted
necklace,
bracelet, and
earrings

by Beth Stone

This decidedly feminine set adds sparkle to any ensemble. The faceted briolettes and nuggets shine like refreshing dew on morning grass, while the pearls' opacity offers striking visual contrast. This trio perfectly accentuates ladylike fashions.

Supply List

necklace
- **10** 14 x 18mm faceted oval beads (Pearlwear, 760-634-7902, pearlwear.com)
- **9** 12mm faceted pear briolettes (Pearlwear)
- **18** 6mm round pearls
- **36** 4mm or 5mm flat spacers
- **4** 3mm round spacers
- flexible beading wire, .014 or .015
- **2** crimp beads
- clasp
- chainnose or crimping pliers
- diagonal wire cutters

earrings
- **2** 12mm faceted pear briolettes
- **2** 6mm round pearls
- **4** 4mm or 5mm flat spacers
- **6** in. (15cm) 22-gauge silver wire, half hard
- pair of earring wires
- chainnose and roundnose pliers
- diagonal wire cutters

bracelet
- **4** 14 x 18mm faceted oval beads
- **3** 12mm faceted pear briolettes
- **6** 6mm round pearls
- **12** 4mm or 5mm flat spacers
- **4** 3mm round spacers
- flexible beading wire, .014 or .015
- **2** crimp beads
- clasp
- chainnose or crimping pliers
- diagonal wire cutters

necklace • 1. Determine the finished length of your necklace. (This one is 17 in./43cm.) Add 6 in. (15cm) and cut a piece of beading wire to that length. String an oval, spacer, pearl, spacer, briolette, spacer, pearl, and spacer. Repeat this pattern until the necklace is within 1 in. (2.5cm) of the desired length, ending with an oval.

2. String a 3mm round, a crimp bead, a round, and half the clasp. Go back through the beads just strung and tighten the wire. Repeat on the other end and check the fit. Add or remove beads, if necessary. Crimp the crimp beads (Basic Techniques, p. 12). Trim the excess wire.

earrings • 1. Cut a 3-in. (7.6cm) piece of wire. String a top-drilled briolette and make a wrap above the bead (Basic Techniques).

2. String a spacer, a pearl, and a spacer. Make a wrapped loop (Basic Techniques) above the spacer. Open the loop on an earring wire and attach the dangle. Close the loop. Make a second earring to match the first.

bracelet • Determine the finished length of your bracelet, add 5 in. (13cm), and cut a piece of beading wire to that length. Follow the necklace directions to make the bracelet. ❖

Contact Beth at (248) 855-9358 or bnshdl@msn.com.

Silver

adornments

by Brenda Schweder

Highlight a three-strand bracelet and earrings with Hill Tribes silver

Hill Tribes silver accents subtle Czech glass in a bracelet with as much whimsy as class. For a fancy (rather than purely functional) finish to this bracelet, look for a box clasp set with a gemstone or mother of pearl.

A

bracelet • **1.** Determine the finished length of your bracelet. (The gray bracelet is 8 in./20cm; the green one, 7½ in./19cm.) Add 5 in. (13cm) and cut three pieces of beading wire to that length. Center the butterfly on one strand.

2. On each side of the butterfly, string three Czech glass beads and a 3 x 6mm silver bead. Repeat until the strand is within 2 in. (5cm) of the desired length, ending with a silver bead.

B

3. On another wire, string a mix of silver beads and Czech glass beads until the strand is within 2 in. of the desired length, beginning and ending with a silver bead.

C

4. On the remaining wire, string a silver bead and five cathedral crystals. Repeat until the strand is within 2 in. of the desired length, ending with a silver bead.

D

5. Cut a 4-in. (10cm) piece of 22-gauge wire. Make a wrapped loop (Basic Techniques, p. 12) on one end.

E

6. String a crimp bead, a large-hole spacer, and the wrapped loop over all three strands. Go back through the beads just strung and one of the silver beads and tighten the wires.

7. Repeat steps 5 and 6 on the other end. Check the fit and adjust if necessary. Crimp the crimp beads (Basic Techniques) and trim the excess wire.

F

8. String one wire stem through a beading cone and make the first half of a wrapped loop above the cone. Slide half the clasp into the loop and complete the wraps. Repeat on the other end with the remaining clasp half.

A

B

earrings • 1. String a cathedral crystal, a 3 x 6mm silver bead with 3mm spacers above and below, and a Czech glass bead on individual head pins. Make a wrapped loop above each bead or spacer.

2. Open an earring wire and string each dangle, putting the smallest dangle in front. Close the wire. Make a second earring to match the first. ✤

Supply List

all projects
- chainnose and roundnose pliers
- diagonal wire cutters

gray and blue bracelet
- **20-25** 6 x 12mm Czech glass beads
- **20-25** 6mm cathedral fire-polished crystals
- **15-20** 3 x 6mm Hill Tribes silver beads
- 19 x 22mm Hill Tribes silver butterfly
- **2** beading cones, approx. 8 x 12mm
- **2** 3mm large-hole round spacer beads
- flexible beading wire, .014 or .015
- 8 in. (20cm) 22-gauge silver wire
- **2** crimp beads
- box clasp (Jess Imports, 415-626-1433, jessimports.com)
- crimping pliers (optional)

green and purple bracelet
- **25-30** 5 x 9mm Czech glass beads
- **20-25** 6mm cathedral fire-polished crystals
- **15-20** 3 x 6mm Hill Tribes silver beads
- 19 x 19mm Hill Tribes silver butterfly
- **2** beading cones, approx. 8 x 12mm
- **2** 3mm large-hole round spacer beads
- flexible beading wire, .014 or .015
- 8 in. 22-gauge silver wire
- **2** crimp beads
- box clasp (Jess Imports)
- crimping pliers (optional)

earrings
- **2** Czech glass beads, 6 x 12mm or 5 x 9mm
- **2** 6mm cathedral fire-polished crystals
- **2** 3 x 6mm Hill Tribes silver beads
- **4** 3mm flat spacers (optional)
- **6** 1½-in. (3.8cm) decorative head pins
- pair of earring wires

Brenda offers kits for the gray and blue bracelet. Contact her at Miss Cellany Jewelry Kits, BrendaSchweder.com.

Flexible fashion

Alter a finished necklace to make a dressy new design

by Paulette Biedenbender

Supple, colorful, neoprene necklaces are gaining a devoted following. Unlike rubber, this material won't tarnish sterling silver. Neoprene's compatibility with silver makes it a perfect base for hanging charms, letter beads, or a pendant. Try taking a finished necklace to a new level by reusing the original clasp and adding connector bars, a few extra findings, and a handful of beads that suit your style. You'll have a funky, fashionable, flexible necklace that's all your own.

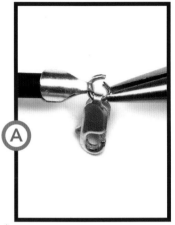

black necklace • 1. Remove the jump rings (Basic Techniques, p. 12) and the clasp from each end of the necklace and set aside.

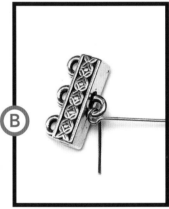

2. Trim the head off a head pin. Make the first half of a wrapped loop (Basic Techniques) at one end. Attach it to a connector bar's single loop.

3. Complete the wraps and string two 4mm flat spacers on the wire.

4. Make the first half of a wrapped loop ⅛ in. (3mm) above the spacer. Attach the loop to one end of the necklace and complete the wraps. Repeat steps 2 through 4 on the other end.

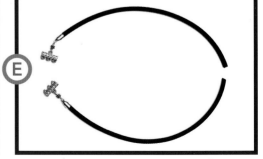

5. Fold the necklace and cut it in half.

248

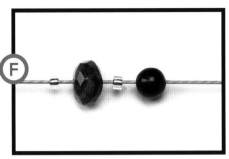

6. Cut three 8-in. (20cm) pieces of flexible beading wire.

To make the inner strand, string a Japanese cylinder bead, a rondelle, a cylinder bead, and a 4mm round. Repeat this pattern for 3½ in. (9cm), ending with a cylinder bead.

To make the outer strand, string the pattern for 4¼ in. (11cm). Tape all the ends and set aside.

Supply List

both necklaces
- flexible beading wire, 014 or .015
- GS Hypo cement
- chainnose and roundnose pliers
- diagonal wire cutters
- scissors
- split ring pliers (optional)

black necklace
- 16-in. (41cm) finished neoprene necklace, 4mm diameter (Art Gems Inc., 800-408-0032, artgemsinc.com)
- 16-in. strand 3 x 5mm faceted rondelles, sodalite
- 16-in. strand 4mm round beads, Botswana agate
- 1g size 11º Japanese cylinder beads
- **12** 2mm round spacer beads
- **4** 4mm flat spacers

- **2** three-to-one connector bars, 10 x 15mm
- **2** 2½-in. (6.4cm) head pins
- **6** crimp beads
- 5mm split ring
- **2** 5mm round crimp ends

pink necklace
- 16-in. (41cm) finished neoprene necklace, 4mm diameter (Art Gems Inc.)
- 8-in. (20cm) strand 4mm faceted round Czech crystals
- 1g size 8º seed beads
- 1g size 11º seed beads
- **12** 2mm round spacer beads
- **4** 4mm flat spacers
- **2** three-to-one connector bars, 10 x 12mm
- **2** 2½-in. head pins
- **6** crimp beads
- 5mm split ring
- **2** 5mm round crimp ends

7. To make the middle strand, string a Japanese cylinder bead, a 4mm round, a cylinder bead, and a rondelle. Repeat this pattern for 3¾ in. (9.5cm), ending with a cylinder bead. Tape one end of the beading wire.

8. On the middle strand, string a 2mm round spacer bead, a crimp bead, a spacer bead, and the middle loop of a connector bar. Go back through the beads just strung. Remove the tape from the other end and repeat. Tighten the wire, but do not crimp the crimp beads.

9. Repeat step 8 on the inner and outer strands, attaching the strands to their respective loops.

Make sure the strands hang evenly between the connector bars. If necessary, remove an equal number of beads on each end to adjust the strands. Crimp the crimp beads (Basic Techniques) and trim the excess wire.

....

pink necklace • **1.** Follow steps 1 through 5 of the black necklace.

2. Follow steps 6 and 7 of the black necklace, substituting a size 11º seed bead for the size 11º Japanese cylinder bead, a size 8º seed bead for the 4mm round, and a faceted crystal for the faceted rondelle.

3. Follow steps 8 through 11 of the black necklace to finish the pink necklace. ✤

10. Check the fit. (These necklaces are 20 in./51cm, including the 4¼-in./11cm beaded section.) Trim an equal length of neoprene from each end, if needed. Glue the inside of the crimp end. Slide it on one end of the necklace. Gently squeeze the sides of the end crimp. Repeat on the other end.

11. On one end, reattach and close the jump ring with the clasp. Repeat on the other end, substituting a split ring for the jump ring with the clasp.

Contact Paulette in care of BeadStyle.

Classic cloisonné

Contrasting colors and textures merge in a cinnabar and cloisonné necklace • **by Adele Droblas**

The cloisonné technique involves soldering metal wires to a copper base, filling in the cells with an enamel paste, and firing the beads. More enamel is applied, and the beads are fired again and polished to a luster. The painstaking enameling and firing process yields beads with vibrant colors – a good match to an intricately carved cinnabar pendant. A simple stringing arrangement showcases the beads without detracting from their rich colors and textures.

1. With roundnose pliers, turn a small spiral at the end of a 5-in. (13cm) piece of 22-gauge wire. Bend the wire upward at the end of the spiral. String the cinnabar pendant onto the wire.

2. Make a wrapped loop (Basic Techniques, p. 12) approximately ½ in. (1.3cm) above the bead. Make sure the loop is perpendicular to the spiral and the wraps continue down to the bead.

3. Determine the finished length of your necklace. (These are 16 in./41cm.) Add 6 in. (15cm) and cut a piece of beading wire to that length. Center the pendant on the wire.

4. On one end, string a seed bead, 5mm round, cloisonné oval, 5mm round, seed bead, barrel, and seed bead on the wire.

5. String a 5mm round, cloisonné oval, 5mm round, seed bead, cloisonné round, seed bead, 5mm round, oval, and 5mm round.

E

6. String a seed bead, 6mm round, seed bead, and cloisonné oval. Repeat three times.

7. Repeat steps 4 through 6 on the other end.

F

8. On one end, string a seed bead, 5mm round, seed bead, 6mm round, three seed beads, a crimp bead, seed bead, and lobster claw clasp. Go back through the seed bead, crimp bead, and three seed beads and tighten the wire. Repeat on the other end, substituting a jump ring for the clasp. Check the fit and adjust as necessary. Crimp the crimp beads (Basic Techniques) and trim the excess wire. ❖

Contact Adele at adele@bonitavida.com or visit her website, bonitavida.com.

Supply List

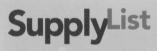

both projects
- flexible beading wire, .014 or .015
- chainnose and roundnose pliers
- diagonal wire cutters
- crimping pliers (optional)

red and blue necklace
- 25 x 38mm cinnabar pendant, vertically drilled
- 14 9 x 11mm oval cloisonné beads, red
- 2 10mm round cloisonné beads, aqua
- 2 11 x 14mm barrel beads, coral
- 10 6mm round beads, blue
- 14 5mm round beads, red
- 1g size 11º seed beads, opaque aqua
- 5 in. (13cm) 22-gauge silver wire
- 2 silver crimp beads
- silver lobster claw clasp and soldered jump ring

red, green, and black necklace
- 25 x 38mm cinnabar pendant, vertically drilled
- 14 9 x 11mm oval cloisonné beads, black
- 2 10mm round cloisonné beads, aqua
- 2 11 x 14mm cloisonné barrel beads, red
- 10 6mm Swarovski pearls, green
- 14 5mm round beads, coral
- 1g size 11º seed beads, beige
- 5 in. 22-gauge gold wire
- 2 gold-filled crimp beads
- gold lobster claw clasp and soldered jump ring

Deck the halls

Make darling holiday dangles

by Mary Krohn, Erica Hipp, and Sydney Smith

Add sparkle to your season with a spunky snowman, twinkling tree, or ethereal angel. Each piece uses just a few beads and components. Whether you present these festive adornments to friends, use them to decorate a special gift, or keep them for yourself, these projects are sure to spark some holiday spirit.

A

B

C

D

snowman • 1. String a 3mm round on a 1-in. (2.5cm) head pin. Make a wrapped loop (Basic Techniques, p. 12), leaving about 2mm between the bead and the wraps.

2. String a flat spacer, an 8mm round, the bead unit from step 1, a 6mm crystal rondelle, 7mm round, 5mm rondelle, and cylinder bead onto a 2-in. (5cm) head pin.

3. Make a wrapped loop above the top bead.

4. Open the loop on an earring wire and attach the snowman. Close the earring wire's loop. Make a second earring to match the first.

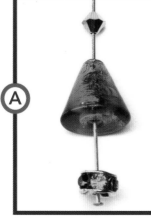

A

B

C

Christmas tree • 1. String a rondelle, cone, and bicone on a head pin.

2. Make a wrapped loop above the top bead.

3. Open the loop on an earring wire and attach the tree. Close the earring wire's loop. Make a second earring to match the first.

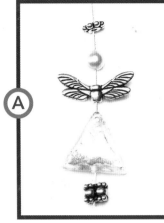

A

B

C

D

E

angel • 1. String a 6mm square spacer or rondelle, a triangle, wings, a round, and a flat spacer on a head pin.

2. Above the top bead, make a wrapped loop large enough to accommodate the ribbon.

3. Determine the finished length of your necklace. (This one is 16 in./41cm.) Add 1 in. and cut a piece of ribbon to that length. Thread the ribbon through the loop and center the pendant.

4. Knot one end of the ribbon and place it in the crimp end. Glue the knot. Fold down the sides of the crimp end (Basic Techniques). Repeat on the other end. Trim the excess ribbon.

5. Attach a split ring to one crimp end and attach a lobster claw clasp to the split ring. Repeat on the other end with just a split ring. ❖

Mary and Erica are employees of Funky Hannah's Beads and Art in Racine, WI; Sydney is Mary's granddaughter. Kits for these projects are available from Funky Hannah's, (262) 634-6088.

Shortcuts

Readers' tips to make your beading life easier

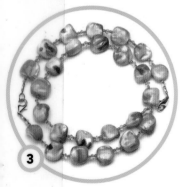

1 branch out
Create wire branches easily by drawing them first. Put the tip of your pencil on a piece of paper. Without lifting the pencil, draw a branch shape and limbs, not crossing any lines. The drawing will give you an idea of what pattern to follow and where to bend the wire.
– Pat Ritter, via e-mail

2 labeling wire
Store wire in a plastic zip-top bag to see its gauge at a glance. Attach a piece of transparent tape to the bag and label the wire gauge, type, and hardness. It's easy to remove the tape and recycle the bag once the wire has been used.
– Grace Carter, Denver, CO

3 extending your options
A bracelet is a handy extender for a necklace; simply finish both pieces with the same size lobster claw clasps and soldered jump rings. To wear, attach the bracelet's clasp to the necklace's jump ring and vice versa. Wear the new length as a long necklace, or wrap it twice for a choker or three times for a chunky bracelet.
– B. Davis, via e-mail

4 scrap storage
Keep empty beading-wire spools to store cut pieces of beading wire. The spool helps the wire retain its shape, free of kinks.
– Christie Nagata, Hilo, HI

5 magnetic personality
Organize findings in metal tins that previously held mints or candles. Attach self-adhesive magnetic tape to the tins and place them on a magnetic bulletin board. (Magnetic tape and bulletin boards are available at office supply stores.) You can also display lists or photos of design ideas.
– Laura Georgy, Quincy, MA